Praise for Hannah Sward

"Hannah Sward's words cut through the niceties of daily life to give us a gritty portrait of what happens to young women when they lose their way. With stark details and incisive language, *Strip* takes readers inside the world of sex work, but not in a salacious way. Rather, hers is the poignant world of lost daughters looking for belonging, hoping to reconnect with missing parents, searching for home and of the lengths to which young women will go to grab hold of redemption."

— Bernadette Murphy, author of
*Harley and Me: Embracing Risk on the Road
to a More Authentic Life*

"Jaw-dropping talent. Hannah Sward is an astonishingly gifted writer whose poetry shines through every sentence. Her ability at depersonalizing herself and making herself into a tragic hero in *Strip* is dizzying. Bottom line is that she is a fine writer who will be heard from."

— Ben Stein, lawyer, economist, actor, author of
How to Ruin Your Financial Life

"Every line, every image Hannah Sward captures is original with her savage wit and the descriptive power she uses to place us in each scene of her bold, devastating adventure. Like a curious witty moth she flickers from the world of stripping, call girl, a menu of drugs and sugar daddies. She dives in, amuses and appalls us, and even in the pits she makes art of each moment. This is no ordinary recovery story. It's a story that defies convention at every step. The writer never feels sorry for herself, she picks up her wit, what's left of her clothes and moves on to a triumphant end where she finds the full creative command of her heritage."

— Jill Schary Robinson, author of
Bed/Time/Story

Strip

Strip

Hannah Sward

Tortoise Books
Chicago, IL

To learning to sit in the hours

Part One: Childhood

The Lonely Beginning
Victoria, BC

My mom left when I was two. While I was in her belly and my dad was standing on his head to find a poem, she'd met a sculptor, Paul. After I came out of her belly, she fell in love with him and didn't want me anymore. All I remember is crawling up on the couch choking on tears, pressing my face and hands to the window, the glass getting cloudy from my breath as I watched her disappear. She didn't see me at the window but maybe if she had she would have come back. But she didn't. It's a good thing my dad wanted me, I love him a lot.

My mom had another baby so I have a half-sister, Rilke, but she feels whole to me. She looks just like Paul, her dad, and everyone says I look like my dad too. I wish I looked like my mom because she is beautiful but she is moving away with Paul and Rilke to Florida where there are alligators. There's a going-away party outside, flowered skirts, bare feet. Rilke steps on broken glass with that little foot of hers. There's too much blood. I put my daisy chain on her ankle. I don't want to tell her I'm not going with her.

Oysters, Blackberries, and Dad's Typewriting
Spring 1975 – Lasqueti Island

Dad and me are living on a houseboat near Victoria, Lasqueti Island. I eat oysters, pick blackberries and brush my teeth with baking soda. Dad forgot toothpaste. There are no stores, cars or other people except my friend Isabel whose parents sail her over on their boat. We roll a log from the shore into the water, hold on and kick our feet. We are naked. On the log we kick, wave our arms, staying steady even when the water gets wavy.

Some days I climb the big rocks while Dad writes. If I can't hear the *click click* of the typewriter, I know I've gone too far. There are foxes and maybe bears in the forest. I don't go into the forest alone, only with Dad. When he comes with me into the forest, he takes my hand into his. I feel so safe, I want to walk with him forever into the forest of sounds and for him to never let go of my hand. Those are my favorite days.

We eat oatmeal and when Dad rolls up his pants and walks into the water, he catches slimy, pretty oysters and crabs to eat. He lays them on the sand, goes back for more. Sometimes the oysters give us pearls and I set them on the windowsill. We squeeze lemons for lemonade, pick blackberries in the bushes, come back with purple-stained fingers.

Dad is on the shore, cross-legged with his black journal on his lap, pen in hand. I sit on the edge of the dock, feet in the water, and I have my own journal on my lap. I write in mine every day just like he does. His eyes are fixed on the clear gray, blue water. Shades of darkness, ripples, then smooth, ripples again.

I like night on the houseboat. I lay on the dock. So many stars, the sky gets all glittered up like it's going out dancing.

Lady Bird Poet
Fall 1975 – Victoria

Today I stayed home from kindergarten. Strep throat. Even
though I can't hardly swallow it's kind of a good thing because
those kids at school, they don't like me. If I could have packed
peanut butter and jelly sandwiches on white bread in metal lunch
boxes I'd probably have friends. Dad packs me tofu and dates in
a paper bag, sometimes liver that I flush down the toilet.

I've laid in my orange bed almost all day listening to my
dad *click, click, bing, clack, clack* on the typewriter. He must've
been writing a poem that was already in his head, cause I don't
hear him stop. I see him with his poems in his head. When we're
together and I ask him something and he won't answer, that means
he's got poems in his head. He just pulls out his pad of paper,
writes something down, this is always how it goes.

He made me hot apple cider vinegar with lots of honey. I like
it when he leaves the honey in its plastic bear next to my bed and
I can squeeze so much that I empty the bear's belly.

I don't remember falling asleep but when I wake up there is

this lady who looks like a bird standing over me. Not the kind of bird that sings in the morning or a hummingbird or even an ordinary pigeon. More like a hungry bird that could just fly right at you, peck you in the face with its beak.

Dad says this ladybird writes poetry and stories too. I don't know anything about her stories, never heard her at any of my dad's readings, but she looks at me and I look at her and I think this is what a lady writer looks like. I am glad I don't want to be a writer cause she doesn't look too happy but I wouldn't probably either if I was all alone writing words. It's a real good thing I want to be an actress and a dancer and if any stories do come up into my head, I'll dance them away.

Ketchup and Iowa

Dad and me are taking the train very far to Iowa. It's an important place for writers. We have sleeping bunks. I get lonely on the train and I wish Rilke were here, she could sleep with me on the top bunk. We'd have to be very tight together though, so no one falls off.

In the morning I look out the window. It must be almost Iowa because there is not so much to see, just snow for miles and miles. I fall asleep and when I wake up there's trees and towns and cows in the snow.

I heard they grow potatoes. I don't like potatoes except with ketchup on them. Ketchup reminds me of this reading Dad ends up doing in Iowa. So many people there some have to stand up. They wait and wait but he isn't anywhere. He was hit by a car on the way to the reading and had to get fixed up at the hospital. After, with his head wrapped in a white bandage stained with blood he walks onstage to read his poems. I imagine when I dance and have a big recital and get hit on the way I'll be just like my dad and show up to dance.

Summer in Sarasota Where I Dance
Summer 1976 – Florida

This is my first summer in Florida. The city where my mom, Rilke, and Paul live is called Sarasota and they live on a street named after a flower, Wisteria. When I get there she tells me that her and Paul are not together anymore but they still live in the same house and he will always be my stepdad. I am glad they still live together and do not know why I have to live separate but my mom says not to worry because every summer she will send for me.

Sometimes friends come over and Mom answers the door with her big boobs all out there. Other times she lays on tinfoil in the backyard topless, blonde hair all spread out. Paul takes Rilke and me to ballet and jazz class at Bunni Wilson's.

"Drop us off in the back," I tell him.

I don't want anyone seeing Rilke and me in Paul's white truck. It's full, with paintings and statues of naked ladies with big bronze bums, arched backs, and no heads.

Rilke and me practice Bunni Wilson's dance routine. Tap, ballet, and jazz. We rehearse in black-and-white wigs in Bunni's pink and black painted studio. Rilke can do five backbends. If I could do them down the school hall, I'd be popular like Rilke and stop hiding under the bleachers at lunch.

At the end of the summer there's a recital at The Pink Elephant, all the seats are filled. For the show we wear glittery pink and silver dresses. We pose for each other. Someday we'll look better, have boobs and hips. We smile into the mirror, laugh, link arms and go onto the stage. Tap, ballet, and jazz. We'll be in movies, dancing onstage. Tap, ballet, and jazz. Everybody will know us.

When I have to leave Florida Rilke grabs my leg and we clutch each other's hands, spin around, then hold each other and cry. I won't see her again until next summer.

My New Russian Mom

When I get back from Florida, Dad starts having meditation groups at home. One Sunday a guru wrapped in orange arrives. He sits on a wood platform with his big orange belly. Bowls of red rose petals are set at his feet. I don't like this man called guru. He pinches my cheeks, gives me a pillow that says Om, and I want to throw that pillow out. It's hard to sit there all quiet with your eyes closed. I want to scratch my feet, try not to. I open one eye. A lady with gray curly hair, big amber stones around her neck, opens both her eyes. We look at each other. She winks. I shut my eyes.

After that he comes every Sunday. Sometimes when everyone's eyes are closed I hide in the closet with a banana and my monkey Pushkin. I want to be outside with Emily eating the good food at her house like Frosted Flakes with whole milk. No tofu.

❀

A couple of months after Dad starts meditation group, I am in the closet with banana peels. I do not want to see Dad's new lady, Alina. He met her at a reading and now she lives with us. She has big blue eyes, dark Russian skin, and a space between her front teeth.

Alina does not want to be my mom.

"I be your sister," she says.

I want to tell her I already have a sister and there's no more room in me for more.

Alina is an artist. Sits on the edge of her chair like she wants to leave. She is stitching cloth dolls. Squints her eyes, threads needle, stitch, stitch, stitch. Russian dolls with no arms and orange red wooly hair flying in all directions. She takes me to her art class, sets me up in the corner with my own little easel. A naked man stands in the middle of the room, hand on hip, leg to side, holding the pose for a long time. Alina moves her charcoal fast across a big sheet of white paper. I try to copy her. Hers looks just like the naked man. Mine is a big black mountain.

It's my birthday. I wake up and my room is filled with lavender, pink, and yellow roses. Alina picked them in the night from the neighbor's yards. My dad calls her honey bear. I imagine big bear Russian feet running across the neighbor's lawn soft as paws. Pick, pick, pick.

Dad likes meditation and guru so much that one day he says to Alina and me, "We are going to India."

We got shots, my arms are itchy. Dad is in his writing studio with the guru. When Alina brings him borscht he says he needs to go to India alone.

Alina stares at guru. "This is your idea."

She pours borscht on guru's orange wrapping, the colors go together. But Dad still goes, leaving us. I don't feel good, not one bit. I sleep in his bed. It is still his bed even though Alina sleeps in it too. I get sick, throw up, and now Alina is mad at me. She tells me to clean up and go to my own bed.

The Man in the Brown Car

1976 – Victoria

I spend so much time alone. I hide under the front porch and watch the cherry blossom petals float to the ground. Alina is at art class and Dad is in India. I like to walk to the park, step in puddles with feet bare in red sandals and feel the water between my toes.

Today, nobody is in the park, not even Emily. Her mom would not let her go today. I swing on the swing with my doll and go so high. A man in a brown car parks across the street under a beautiful tree that has not lost its leaves. He watches me, waves for me to come over. I keep swinging. He waves again. I get off the swing, walk towards him, hold my doll tight.

I am in his car. He tells me he is bringing me home but he drives so far and my feet are cold and I start crying. He stops the car at the end of a street in front a yellow 'Dead End' sign.

"Do you know how babies are made?" he asks.

I know they come from bellies but I can't talk. I am wearing pink- and white-checkered shorts. The doors are locked and his zipper goes down and his stomach has hair on it and it's white and there's more hair down there. He takes out a thing like a floppy fish and my shorts are off. The fish goes stiff. He's so close to me and I can't breathe.

"Stop the crying," he says. He tugs and tugs on the thing and it's touching me down there. "If you tell anyone I will kill you."

I hold my doll's hand so tight and try to hold my breath so I don't cry and close my eyes.

"Open them," he says. "Look down."

So much white stuff comes out of the fish and it's all over me. He tells me again if I tell anyone he will kill me.

I can't stop crying and I know that is not good. "I promise, I won't."

He drives around and around and my shorts are back on but they don't feel good. They are wet like my feet. He brings me back to the park and the brown car goes away. I am not dead. My doll has lost her shoe.

I am at the police station and my clothes and my doll are in plastic bags. I don't know how I got there and I am so scared because all I can think is he will come back to kill me if he knew I told but I don't remember telling or how I got here but I am sitting with Alina and she is not happy with me. She is mad. We get in the police car and drive and drive and look for the man in the brown car. It gets dark and Alina brings me home. I don't want my dad in India and my mom in Florida. I just want them to come home.

Big Nightmares and My Monkey Pushkin

I pee my pants a lot and have big nightmares about having a baby. I try to keep my eyes open all night and hold onto my monkey, Pushkin. He's made of gray wool socks and has very long legs and arms that can wrap around me. There's a monkey tree out my window but I never see monkeys in it, they are probably waiting for the bananas to grow. Dad is back from India and he said that could take a very long time.

When I do shut my eyes my belly grows so big in the night and I walk in my sleep to my dad's and Alina's room. I lay on the itchy rug on my back, put my knees up with my feet on the floor and I cry and push so hard. There is a baby in me and it won't come out. I know I do this because when I wake up that's where I am and I'm all sweaty and there is no baby in me anymore but every night when my eyes go shut the baby comes back. When I go to my room Pushkin is on the floor with his legs all spread out.

Dad picks me up from school at lunchtime and we go to the doctors. So many days of school I miss. In a small white room with a metal bed I have to go to sleep and it is very hard. I don't want to and I cry. A lady sticks wires in my head and Dad says he will be there when I wake up and that the lady needs to watch my brain when I go to sleep.

When I wake up the lady gives me a lollipop, a different color every time. When I get to purple and have had every color of the rainbow the nightmares go away.

I ask my dad, "What did they do to my head to make them go away?"

He says he doesn't know. Nobody talks about the man in the brown car and I don't either, not even to Emily or Pushkin. I don't want to get in trouble and if he ever gets into my head, I will push him away.

Buttercup Hill

Emily and me take turns playing doctor lying naked. All her dolls on shelves look down at us. I have one doll but she is still at the police station in a plastic bag and she has only one shoe. She lost it in the park but I don't go back there because I don't like parks or swinging anymore.

After we play doctor all of Emily's friends come over for her seventh birthday. So many balloons float to the ceiling with curled ribbons hanging down, all the colors make me think of lollipops and I almost start to cry. Emily opens her presents in her pink bedroom on the third floor. All the girls gather around. She opens a big one wrapped with a yellow bow. It's a porcelain doll with eyelashes that blink. She passes it around and then we all start playing, running around the room. When no one is looking, I turn out the light and everyone screams. It is night and dark. I grab her new doll and throw it out the window. The doll is cracked open on the pavement its legs all spread out. Nobody knows I did it. I never tell.

Emily and me go to Buttercup Hill. That hill has lots of buttercups, tulips and lavender. The white house with broken windows has slabs of plywood nailed in the shape of an X, it sits there empty. We lie down in the grass, slide our fingers along the lavender, pick stems, tie them together and make flower crowns on our heads. We walk on tippy toes, pretending we are fancy ladies with perfume smelling all good, talking about what we are going to be when we grow up.

Now we don't go there anymore. A girl in our class got killed on that hill and nobody knows how it happened. Her hands were tied and she had no pants on. Maybe it was the man in the brown car and he showed her how babies were made too and then he killed her.

The Orange Guru
1977 – Victoria

My dad and Alina have this kind of wedding in an ashram with the orange guru who sent my dad to India. There is a circle of men and women all getting married at the same time. They hold hands and make offerings to one another. Women sit in lotus position with bare feet, rings on their toes, bells on their ankles and a red dot of a third eye. Men kneel down to them, dressed in loose white open shirts and white drawstring pants. Cymbals come together, everyone stands, then me and other children circle parents with an incense stick.

My dad takes Alina's hand in his, puts a silver ring with a tiger's eye on her finger. They are married, everyone is married. Hands lock, chanting, more cymbals. All the brides dancing in saris threaded with gold, burgundy, magenta, marigold.

Thin men in white turbans offer trays of tofu, brown rice, tamari and mangoes. Later, men sit crossed legged across the room from the women, I sit next to Alina, we cross our legs too. A microphone is passed around and people ask the orange guru questions.

"What is it to be in the here and now?"

My feet fall asleep. I want to erase the red dot in between guru's eyes, take the microphone, and say 'fuck you'. I know words like that. I look down at the soles of Alina's brown feet with anklets. All the veins in them rise above the skin, look alive but there's something about those feet I like. They look like part of the earth, not pale and flimsy with unchipped pink polish.

In the middle of the questions I go to the bathroom in my pants. No one told me not to drink water after the food. Alina makes me wash out my pants. I cry. Wear a yellow sari with no underpants. My clothes are hung out to dry and I just want to go home. What is my real mom doing in Florida? Maybe if I was with her—I don't know. I don't know.

Flying Cockroaches
Summer 1977 – Florida

There are flying cockroaches and no air conditioning in the Florida house on Wisteria. The old Spanish windows and sliding glass doors are left open. Rilke and me drag our beds down the wood stairs, move the dining room table to the side, and sleep under the ceiling fan. Sometimes we sleep on top of the table so we are closer to the fan.

Rilke likes to kiss the length of my arm before we go to sleep. Most of the time I let her, flopping my skinny pale arm over her pillow. Kiss, kiss, kiss. Like she is the prince and me a princess.

During the day, we sit on eggs in a bucket and wait for them to hatch, or we invite the neighbor girl over to play dentist. When we stop liking her and want her to disappear, we brush her teeth with Head and Shoulders shampoo. Her parents don't let her come back.

A Baby Brother Appears
Fall 1977 – Victoria

When I get back from Florida, Alina has a big belly like the guru's. I watch it grow and her feet too, they get extra wide from all that weight.

"You have baby brother soon," she tells me.

I want to have a baby brother even though I never want my belly to grow big and to have a baby but when Alina has my brother I will push him in the pram down the street. Not to the park. I do not go there alone, not anymore and if my brother gets any ideas about going there alone when he can walk, I won't let him.

Alex, the baby that's now my brother, he came out of Alina's stomach. He's got a very red face, fat cheeks, squinty eyes, and white hair that sticks up in all directions. I try and flatten it but it doesn't want to go down. He came home in a yellow blanket with blue ducks stitched on the edges. He's kind of sweaty and smells like chicken but not in a bad chicken way.

Dad puts Alex in a green canvas carrier on his back just like he did with me when I was very little. We go to so many poetry readings, Alex always falls asleep.

Alina calls Alex her son but does not call me her daughter. One day maybe she will change her mind. Like we'll be walking down the street and someone will say, "And who is this pretty little girl?" Alina will tell them I am hers. Then I would really have two moms, one for winter and one for summer when it's very hot and there's flying cockroaches. I wonder if they fly somewhere else in the winter. I hate winter, just too cold.

I don't think Alex will like winter either but if he's bundled up real good maybe he won't even notice. He already doesn't like a whole lot of things. His crib is in my room, he cries all the time and I can't hardly sleep. I wish he had his own room. Sometimes I get so upset I want to throw my piggy bank against the wall with all that crying but I don't. I would have to clean up all the pennies in the morning. I also know it would not make Alex cry any less.

Hidden in a Sari
Winter 1978 – Victoria

My dad is out reading his poems at a bookstore and I don't know where Alina is. Alex and me have a boy babysitter.

"I don't like that boy," I tell my dad and Alina.

They don't ask any questions when I tell them. Maybe they didn't hear me but I am scared to tell them again because I don't want to get in trouble with Alina like I did with the man in the brown car, and if they ask questions I wouldn't know what to say anyway. He keeps coming back and I want him gone. I want us to move away and be so far from him.

He is in high school and has too-small eyes, pimples, and bushy hair. He likes to play games with clothes off but I like clothes on and tell him but he doesn't listen. Alex sleeps in his crib and I try to be so quiet and not wake him up. He's just a baby and I don't want anything to happen to him and when he gets older I will make sure he never plays these kinds of games.

"Today we are going to play hide and seek," the boy babysitter says. "The rule is if I find you by the time I count to twenty sheep you must be tickled and then I touch you. Now take off all your clothes."

He closes his eyes. "One sheep…"

I run into my closet and get a red sari with gold threading that my dad brought me back from India. I wrap it around me and go so fast on my tip toes down the stairs into the basement where it is dark and I get flat on the floor and slide under a couch not anyone big could fit. I hear him upstairs.

"Hmmm, where could she be?"

I pull the sari over my head. He's opening the basement door and his feet are heavy coming down the stairs.

"Twelve sheep, thirteen…"

I want to crawl out a window and run so far away. I am so scared, I think of my mom and Rilke. I want to be in Florida. Maybe if I tell my mom she will want me and I can move to Florida not just for summer but maybe not. Maybe she would not even send for me in July because I am dirty now. That's what the babysitter says, I am a dirty girl.

The sari smells like my dad when I sit behind him on his Raleigh bicycle as he pedals through the woods. My dad wears a red beret that has a purple sequined heart stitched on, and a tweed jacket that itches when I put my face on his back. My two braids fly out behind us. I want him to come home.

Bobby Socks & Patent Heels

Summer 1979 — Florida

Rilke and me walk home from dance class down Osprey Avenue in the Florida sun, kicking the daisy bushes. When we get home, Mom is sitting on the bed in a pinstriped workman's shirt, bare legs and pearl toenail polish. She is combing a little girl's hair, making it look very pretty, pulling it back into a high ponytail with a purple scrunchie.

"This is Kim-Ly," Mom tells us. "She lives down the street."

Kim-Ly is from Vietnam and she lives with her mom and two sisters. She sits there at the edge of our mom's bed in a pink ruffled dress and white socks, the kind with frills around the ankles and black patent leather shoes with a silver buckle.

Rilke and me stand in the doorway of our mother's large airy room. A six-foot-high abstract painting, done in soft, pastel colors, hangs above the bed. An antique writing desk on the left, a turquoise pottery vase on it. Old Mediterranean-style windows open, a long ballet bar on another wall, palm trees outside, and Kim-Ly.

I don't remember Mom doing my hair. There's a picture of

her French-braiding Rilke's. I'm standing kind of to the side, watching. Four inches taller than Rilke with a pageboy haircut, a too-small Mickey Mouse dress and I'm feeling ugly. I always feel ugly next to Rilke, I don't think she feels that way next to me.

After that, Kim-Ly visits our mom too much. Mom loves that little girl, asking her questions about Vietnam and when is her dad coming to Florida. Kim-Ly likes watching our mom brush her own hair and get ready to see whatever man she is going to see. Rilke and me go to our bedroom, close the door, and watch *The Beverly Hillbillies*. We lay outside with tinfoil all around us, wait for the sun to turn us brown, and wait for Kim-Ly to leave. The sun never turns us brown, only red, and Kim-Ly, she sticks around for too long.

Rilke and me have women in our life, where we are their version of Kim-Ly. Anna Alexander, a beautiful Greek actress with dark red hair. She always wears Cherries in the Snow Revlon lipstick and she drives a yellow convertible VW Bug. She tells us, "Men fell out of trees for me when I was younger."

I hope they fall out of trees for me one day. Anna is our acting teacher at Florida Studio Theater, where Rilke and me go to theater camp. We go every summer since we want to be actresses. There are lots of little girls and boys and everybody loves Anna but after camp is over for the day and parents are picking up their Pavarotti-singing sons and tapdancing daughters, Rilke and me go off with Anna in her yellow Bug. We spend nights with her, read *Diary of Anne Frank* and eat baklava.

Sometimes Anna picks us up at our house on Wisteria. We hear the tires of her Bug crunching the gravel, and out we run. Mom stands by the door, watching us climb into Anna's backseat in matching gold lamé shorts and heart-shaped sunglasses. It seems like Mom doesn't want us to leave but we go off any way with Anna and her Cherries in the Snow lipstick.

There's also Bunni, our dance teacher. She only wears pink and black and I've never seen her without either a black or white spiky wig. Her house has black- and pink-checkered marble floors, a winding pink staircase, a pool with a mermaid spitting water, and she even has a pink poodle that we take for walks and a husband who we never see. I'm pretty sure he must love her on account of that house, and that she's a really good dancer.

Bunni takes us out for dinner at fancy old-man restaurants. We dress up in wigs and white gowns with matching sequined gloves, and the men with their gray hair and red and blue ties stare.

Bunni tells us, "Order whatever you like, girls."

We copy her and order shrimp scampi that we pretend to like, and hot chocolate lava soufflé with raspberries that we do like.

It's good, being with Anna and Bunni. We go home, feeling something close to special.

The Witches' House
Winter 1980 – Toronto, Algonquin Island

We move across the whole of Canada from Victoria to Algonquin Island. I'm not sure why, but this is a very good thing, I will be so far from the boy babysitter. There are no stores or cars, only a fire truck and a milkman.

I am in fourth grade. No kids like to come over because our place is called the Witches' House. Jars of weeds on the shelves, mice crawling in between the fluorescent pink insulation and the plastic, iron-clawed bathtub in the kitchen, stinky outhouse-type hole in the ground for a bathroom, a swing in the living room that if you swing on it you swing into the wood stove. My bed is made out of a piece of plywood, set up on stilts close to the ceiling. I climb a ladder to get in. That bed is full of yellow chalk dust. Most nights I sneeze and can't sleep, so I watch these mice scramble around in the insulation. One time, it snows so hard that the roof in my room falls in and I wake up covered in snow.

So next, I move into the little loft in the living room. There is a wood ladder leading up to it a few feet from the wood stove. I feel safe there like in the closet. I paint a rainbow on the ceiling and I have an aqua plastic record player, play "Another One Bites the Dust" over and over. My monkey Pushkin is here, in the move he lost an eye but he still feels fine to me.

On this Algonquin Island, you have to know somebody to find a better place, so Alina gets a paper route in order to get to know the Islanders. To protect her fur coat from the snow, she turns it inside out and paints the lining with a woman who has red hair that sweeps around wild, like the dolls she stitches. She delivers *The Toronto Star* to two hundred and fifty houses wearing that coat with her fur hat.

Soon we move from the witches' place to a house on Wyandot. Everything we have is in a big wood wagon. It is hard for my dad and Alina to push it to the new house across icy patches, with strong wind blowing from the lake. I am huddled with Pushkin in the wagon and frozen spider plants.

The two-story green house has a real bathroom. Alina paints the window frames red, hangs her etchings. Dad has a writing studio with a skylight. I bring him Sleepytime tea with the honey bear. I want him sleepy so he'll come inside, not write so much. Sometimes I bring my journal into his studio, I sit on the floor next to his feet, and we write poems together.

I win a star-shaped cake at school for my own poem about missing Rilke. Dad throws the cake into the compost heap. He doesn't like me to eat sugar but I like candy and start sticking Butterfinger bars down my pants when we go to the store in the city. A lady with a pointy nose shakes her finger at me, back and forth. I see that fat finger every time I steal a chocolate bar.

On my way to ballet class, I steal nice new pink tights like the other girls have, with a seam down the back. I don't get to ballet class that day, I'm arrested, but not fingerprinted on account of being nine. Dad spanks me. He tells me he does not want to, but that Alina said it would teach me a lesson. It doesn't. If I get spanked again I will put a book in the back of my pants.

That night Alina says, "Until spinach is finished, you stay at table."

I don't like spinach. Somehow I get that spinach into the pockets of my green corduroys and I'm excused and go to my bedroom. I have a piggy bank that's a black-and-white cat with a long neck and pink whiskers. I stuff that spinach into that piggy bank cat through the hole in the bottom where you get the pennies out.

On Sundays, Alina, me and Alex wheel the red bundle buggy down Oneida and Dakota, across the bridge, along the lagoon, past the fire station and the Candy Lady's house, to the ferry docks. Other Islanders are there with their bundle buggies, holding their kids hands, watching the ferry cross Lake Ontario with Toronto, the whole city behind it. The CN Tower, Harbor Bay, all the tall and jagged buildings. We are taking the ferry into the city to the St. Lawrence Market.

Dad gives us fifty dollars, Alina asks for more. Sometimes we get fifty-five or sixty and buy almond pastries with marzipan centers at the French bakery, eat them as we walk past whole chickens roasting on metal sticks, skinned pigs hang from rope, baskets of yellow and red tomatoes, bundles of parsley gathered together with rubber bands, cabbage and radishes.

"Steak, steak, a dollar ninety-eight," a man wearing a blood-stained apron shouts out.

Seven men with long black braided hair play the flute. Sometimes I can't swallow my pastry because the music is so beautiful. Today I put a box of strawberries in the open flute case with the dollar bills and quarters so they'd know I saw them and that I wish I had money to put in the case.

Today, walking through that market, Alina picks out cranberry beets. She strings them on the sides of the bundle buggy, the long beet necks hanging down next to the cauliflower and chicken. I don't know how but even with just fifty dollars that buggy is always full.

It's the end of the day. Alex is sleepy and I try to carry him but it's too far so I just take his dirty warm hand in mine. It's real important that he knows I love him even though I can't carry him all the way.

Rhinestones and Lizards
Summer 1982 – Florida

Last summer, when I was visiting Florida, Mom was working as an interior designer at a department store, Burdines. Every morning she wore coral polish and nude panty hose to work. Every morning seemed like a lot to her and it did to me too.

After she quits she says, "The worst two years of my life. I used to lock the door of my office and take a nap under the desk. I was always being told to sell more couches to my clients to decorate their homes, but I couldn't bring that ugliness into someone's home."

Now she paints tee shirts. She buys packs of twenty shirts at Woolworth's and lays them out on the grass in the backyard. She says she feels free working out there in a man's button-up shirt, all bare underneath. I like watching those little, shapely legs now bare from pantyhose as she moves across the lawn. She paints those shirts fast taking a square sponge, sticking it in the paint, wringing it out, and pressing it on the shirt. She'll have fifty shirts waiting to dry in maybe thirty minutes. While she waits for the shirts to dry, she takes out a box of rhinestones.

Each shirt has six, that's a lot of rhinestoning.

Rilke and I watch her often enough so we learn how to do it. One afternoon Mom goes to see Marco, her lover, and she has the shirts all piled up leaving them to rhinestone the next day. We decide to surprise her and take the six rhinestones we'd need for each shirt and stick the metal circle under the shirt so the spikes poke through. Then we press the rhinestones into place, making sure each one is set firm. I guess we had enough Yahtzee and roller skating on the lanai that day, or maybe we were just feeling extra loving or we thought she'd love us more if we rhinestoned, but when she got home all fifty shirts were sparkling. She said she liked that very much, it made her happy. It was nice to be part of a job she liked.

She is good at selling shirts because she is from New York and people from New York are good at getting people to buy things, except unattractive furniture from department stores.

I am not from New York and don't think I am good at selling anything.

Most of the time, after each blast of fury painting, she washes her thick hair, puts on her makeup, and lies on the bed real still waiting for Marco to call. Sometimes he does and she leaves all those painted shirts that are set on the lawn waiting to dry and by the time she gets home they are.

One time, when she is at his place, Rilke and I are swinging close together in the hammock. We watch the lizards have sex on the screen, one lizard on either side of the screen.

"They sure have a lot of sex," Rilke says. "Kinda like Mom."

When she says that, we get quiet and I feel sad and I think she does too.

"I'll never be like her," I say.

Then there's a lightning bolt, and gray comes over the sky fast the way it does in Florida. We look at all those fifty shirts on the lawn. Then there is thunder and we just lay there in the hammock and we don't make a move to get those shirts and it starts raining real hard, and all the magenta and aqua paint bleeds across the shirts and still we watch. The rain stops. This is what is called a sun shower in Florida. We stare at the paint bleeding into the lawn and don't say anything to each other. We get up from the hammock, put our matching Woolworth's roller skates on, metal wheels to the pavement and we skate away down the street.

The Silent Man with Scorpions in His Hair
1983 – Algonquin Island

Dad is silent on Sundays. He goes to his studio and writes. Alina never seems to get used to it. She sits at the edge of her chair, making fast little angry stitches on her Russian dolls. This one has one cloth leg shorter than the other, three others have no hands or feet but their waists are embroidered with burgundy ribbons and sequins.

I practice ballet, *jeté* across the living room in my pink toe shoes into the kitchen. Dad has come from the studio to make apple cider vinegar with honey. Still silent. Over the potted geraniums in the window above the sink, I see Alex on the sidewalk in his yellow big wheel, pedaling.

The whole family is going to see a guru at a retreat. It is not the orange one.

"This guru lived in India with scorpions in his hair," Dad tells us. "Hasn't talked in thirty years."

Dad left orange guru after it came out the guru had slept with the ladies who sat with bowls of flowers at his feet. This wasn't good because he had been telling people to not do sexual stuff. I don't know why.

I'm sure this retreat is far, I don't know where. We ferry into the city, streetcar to subway. I fall asleep. A lady with a turban drives us down roads with many trees. The retreat is dark except for fireflies and lots of stars.

We go to sleep in a log cabin.

Next comes oatmeal for breakfast outside at long wood tables with lots of other families who have white satchels with Om symbols. Then we gather around the stage, sit on the grass. The new guru Baba sits cross-legged on the stage. He has a long knotted beard so it doesn't get caught in the fat rope he is swallowing inch by inch. Some people sitting on the grass, and my dad, they swallow the rope too.

Now people take teapots out of satchels. An assistant guru walks around pouring salted water from jugs into the teapots. Everybody tilts their heads, pouring water into one nostril, out the other. Trickles of water from forty nostrils feed the grass. Baba hands out lollipops for us kids, they have no sugar but I eat mine anyway.

Someone rings a bell, it is time for people to ask Baba questions.

"What is happiness?" a woman holding a baby asks.

Baba looks at the chalkboard in his lap. Taking a big breath, his belly goes in, then belly out, big. He raises his chalkboard, it is blank. There is a sigh. Some nod, some just look at him.

I run off into a field of weeds, the kind that look like they have a see-through moon on top. I pick one. As I blow the moon away I make a wish then pick more moon weeds and lie in the grass, close my eyes, make blank wishes.

I play hide-and-seek with Alex. Right away I see his feet sticking out behind a wide tree. They look like small potatoes with toes, sturdy feet that can get you places.

"You found me too fast," he says.

So we just lay in this sandbox, arms and legs out like wings. Like in the snow. Only sand angels aren't cold.

Reggie Jackets
Summer 1984 – Florida

Rilke and I are together again, getting in trouble. Sometimes it's for something that isn't our fault like when we're invited to a girl's birthday party. We bring her a cake and she tells everyone that we poisoned it because she gets sick the next day. We didn't poison it. We did make a tray of Rice Krispie treats for one of our mom's boyfriends, though, and mixed the marshmallows with castor oil.

Sometimes Mom goes to the department store and buys us matching things like our Reggie jackets that have patches of fake fur, all shades of brown stuck together. Meant for winter but we are so proud we put that fur on and hand-in-hand we walk down Wisteria in our Reggie's, bare legs, and orange flip-flops.

"If Ryan Howard could see me now," Rilke says.

We always stop at the daisy bush.

"He loves me," we say, picking off one yellow petal at a time. "He loves me not."

If it's a not, we pick more petals until it is yes again.

In the night we ride our banana-seat bicycles down the street or put on our matching Woolworth's roller skates that are red and white with a blue stripe, then skate home and rattle dice all night. Marathon games of Yahtzee. *Rattle, rattle.*

Close to the time when I have to take the airplane home to my dad, we fight. Go to our separate rooms and slam the doors. After a couple of songs—Wham! on high volume behind her door, The Beatles from mine—we sit close to the vent separating us and wait for one of us to talk.

And we always do. She comes into my room and we lay on the bed, her head in my lap or mine in hers. We watch *The Beverly Hillbillies* and talk about how when we are older and done with school, we'll meet in LA so we can be together.

Peeling Avocados for Karma
Winter 1984 – California

Baba, the new guru with the knotted beard, has inspired my dad to move across the continent to the Santa Cruz Mountains to live at his meditation center, Mount Madonna.

In the middle of winter we arrive at the San Francisco Airport dressed in fur hats and wool scarves. A lady in a sari meets us. I don't know if there will be other fourteen-year-olds.

I am given a Sanskrit name Sumitra, it means friends of all. Dad is Jai Per Kash. Even Alina and Alex can't pronounce their new names. We have a cabin with an outhouse up a trail. The first night I stepped on a slug the size of a banana. Now in the night I pee in the bushes. We eat tofu with brown rice, no spices, homemade unsalted granola. I want sugar and meat and to go home.

This first Sunday we go down the mountain to Watsonville to chant and do laundry. Me, my dad, Alex and Alina, get in an avocado-colored Volvo, at every turn down the mountain Dad honks.

Alina is crying, yelling, "We're going to die."

All the big pines are blowing. Alex and me are tossing, hanging onto each other in the back seat. His cheeks too red. I want Alina to be quiet.

"Let's talk about what flavor ice cream we'll get," I whisper to Alex.

"Rocky Road," he says.

Now we pass an old gas station with blue windowpanes. A man with a straw hat sits out front on a milk crate. Stretching behind are strawberry fields where men, women and kids are hunched over picking berries.

Chanting is in the community center near the post office. Outside the post office, men in cowboy boots, blue jeans, leather belts with shiny silver horn buckles spit tobacco juice out of the corner of their mouths. One smiles, his front tooth is silver like his buckle.

All of us from Mount Madonna walk by in white cloth tunics. The cowboys nod. Inside we chant Hari Krishna and then go do our laundry.

Alina is peeling organic black avocados 'for Karma' she says. Everybody helps in the kitchen for Karma. Today I chop extra carrots for good things to happen and the bad things I've done. Alina teaches art here and my dad teaches poetry. Ten of us in the high school. Daya, the only twelfth grader, will have her own graduation ceremony. She'll get to wear a crown and sit in a red and gold throne.

The commune is supposed to be communal, bring families together. But even though Dad's right here next to me eating tempeh in the main room with the long windows overlooking the fog, I feel more separate than ever.

Today I'm making kids' lunches. I'm up at five-thirty when the fog is so thick I have to look at the clock to see it's day. I spread almond butter on forty slices of seven-grain bread, wash apples, wrap sandwiches in Saran Wrap, open a big box of cinnamon granola bars. One in each of the paper lunch bags. Two in mine, maybe three. I feel greedy, like Baba Hari Daas will know. He knows a lot.

The Death of a Cat
Fall 1985 – California, Mount Madonna

Today Alina and Alex didn't come home. Dad and me haven't seen them since this morning from a walk. We walk all around Mount Madonna looking for them.

"She must have gotten a ride into Watsonville to shop," my dad tells me before I go to bed.

Then in the morning Dad is so pale he doesn't look good at all.

Alina left a note under the pillow. She has taken Alex and gone back to the island.

"Back to the island?" I ask. "What are you talking about, can I read the letter?"

In it she says she can't peel one more avocado for Karma and that she has gone back to Toronto with Alex to live with a carpenter who she had been having an affair with before we left. I never saw my dad so upset. It is something terrible and I feel horrible too. All I want to do is to see Alex.

"There was never a time she wasn't sitting on the edge of her chair like she wanted to leave," my dad says.

We fly to Toronto, try to get her to come back. Dad doesn't even get to see Alina. She won't let him but I see her and Alex. Dad gets to see Alex though, and takes him ice-skating.

"Hot chocolate too," Alex says when I bring him back to the carpenter's.

That's where they are living. Alex, with his blonde head of hair and red Russian seven-year-old cheeks. He is happy to see me, I don't know if Alina is. The carpenter, Brett, lives in a Portuguese neighborhood, tall skinny apartments, stuck together. Hot pink, coral, sea blue. Against the white snow the homes and all their colors look like a rainbow at street level but inside nothing rainbow about it. I want to take Alex away with me. Instead I read him Peter Rabbit books, even though he's too old for that. We walk to the corner store, his little chubby hand in mine, I buy him Mars bars. We kick the snow and throw snowballs at each other.

Alex has a fat orange cat.

"His name is Pushkin," he says. "Like your monkey."

He pets that cat, buries him in the snow, big head and orange ears sticking out. Later he brings Pushkin inside, warms him by the stove then goes back outside to play ice hockey on the frozen sidewalk. Alina makes me potato perogies. Alina and Brett start fighting and Brett grabs Pushkin by the tail, throws him against the wall. Blood everywhere. The cat on the floor dead, orange ears turned red with blood. I run to the window. Alex, lips blue from the cold, is hitting the puck from one end of the street to the other. Alina scrubs and scrubs and I wrap Pushkin in a gray wool blanket and go out the back door, down the icy fire escape. I bury him in the snow, go back up the fire escape, kick over a frozen plant, through the apartment, to the front door. Alex has snot frozen beneath his nose, his skates are too big, his ankles cave in. I don't want to leave him with Alina and Brett.

It is time for me to go back to Dad at the hotel. We fly back to California. Just the two of us, alone.

My Father's Women

1986 – California, Santa Cruz

Dad and I don't live at Mount Madonna anymore. We have moved down the mountain to Santa Cruz and my dad has a new girlfriend, Clara. Clara with curly black hair, small brown eyes. A poet but not like any poet I ever met. She has a stinky dog and she doesn't like me. We have moved in with her. I sit on the edge of the bed in my new room that is painted pee yellow. I touch the polyester lace bedspread, the frame of the oval mirror matches the glossy fake dresser. It all makes my eyes water. The dog, Clancy, scratches at the door.

Clara goes shopping at Safeway, pushes the cart, fills it up with biscuits made from a tin tube, Neapolitan ice-cream, a tub of Country Crock margarine that is set on Clara's dinner table.

I think of going to Morton's with Mom and Rilke on Osprey Avenue. We walked down one aisle, Mom said, "I can't do this."

We left the empty cart and went home. Mom gave Rilke and me money to go to Waffle House where we shared a grilled cheese sandwich with ketchup.

I'm looking at myself in Clara's oval mirror. My crew cut hair from the barbershop is not beautiful.

"You look like your father in the navy," my mom says after she sees the picture I sent her.

I tell her I will grow it back by the time I see her next summer.

After I have been in the yellow room for six months Clara joins Weight Watchers, Dad is hired as Santa Claus to make money in between poetry readings. One afternoon Dad and me find this aluminum trailer in the woods. The inside is paneled with real wood and is empty with nothing but leaves, dirt, and cobwebs. We get it hauled to Clara's. I clean it out good. We put in a fold-out table, bed at the bow where I can see the sky in the little window above. I stare up out of that window into the night imagining me and my dad not living with Clara, but somewhere on a boat out at sea.

Before school, I listen to Bob Dylan and Carol King.

Dad knocks on the door. "I guess you're up."

He comes in. I'm sitting on the chair tying my sneakers.

"I don't know why Clara doesn't like me."

"Why do you think she doesn't?" Dad asks.

"I can tell, just the way she looks at me, narrowing her eyes. She can do without me, like you feel about her dog."

"Maybe," he says. "You're competition. I have nothing against Clancy the dog. I just don't want him sleeping in the bed, especially because he smells rotten."

One day I come home from school. Dad sits at the kitchen table, newspaper all laid out, circling ads in the classifieds with a red marker. He looks at me, I look at him.

The red circles around the ads mean we're moving out of Clara's. A week later, we pack everything into Dad's green Volvo and move in with Fran. I think it is a good idea because Fran is a lesbian and Dad won't be sleeping in her bed. Nothing can go wrong.

Fran has short curly hair, wears khaki shorts and Birkenstocks, and doesn't like me any better than Clara. She never says a word to me but quivers her nostrils when I'm around.

We rent rooms in the back of her house, the part that doesn't match the front. It's on a lot of wooded land. Down a path from the backdoor is an octagonal room, windows on all sides from floor to ceiling, that's my room. Every night I sleep in the forest. Sometimes the trees keep me company, other times they make me lonely.

Most of the time, after school and ballet class, I go to 7-Eleven to buy a pint of vanilla bean ice cream, come home and sit on the floor of my room, eating the melting ice cream with a plastic spoon. If it's before a dance recital, I only drink grapefruit juice for three days. Sometimes my friend Daya comes over, we play music, dance around. I spend nights at her house a lot. Her parents want to adopt me. Not for real, but that's what they say.

After three months into living at Fran's, I come home one day. It's raining. I unlock and shut the door behind me. Coming from upstairs I hear Fran groaning, "Robert, oh Robert."

I walk towards the foot of the stairs, hear the rain beat against the window, or is it the bed shaking? I stop in front of the mantle, look at a glass unicorn set on top of a book. It makes me think of curtains with frills. I pick up the unicorn, two horns, I break one horn off and put it in my pocket. Put the one-horned unicorn back.

Dad comes into my room one night two weeks later, he

seems weird. "I don't think you'll need to, but just in case, you know how to call 911."

I figure we'll be leaving. Next day I take a red marker and the paper, bring it to my room, and circle classifieds with no lady.

This new apartment we moved into is just ours, no lady around. There's a swimming pool in the middle of the courtyard that no one swims in, not even me. Dad sleeps on a futon in the living room, I'm in the bedroom with all of Dad's books and a slit of a window.

It's a few months later. A dating service has hired Dad to write an article for *Good Times* newspaper.

"They asked if I'd like to go on a date," he tells me. "It's a fancy dating service. The people who sign up pay more money than our rent for a month. I said no."

"I think you should try it."

It's not so good seeing Dad alone.

"Just once," I say, lifting my finger. "We don't have to live with her."

The service matches him with Miriam, a fiftysomething Jewish woman from Chicago who was married for thirty years, graduated from Berkeley, is an artist, and has three grown children.

Dad goes off in his car with flowers, chocolates and a copy of his latest novel, *A Much Married Man*.

"Maybe leave the book," I say.

He takes it anyway.

I lay down on the bright green shag carpet in the living room.

Too shaggy, like the carpet needs to be mowed. The cottage cheese ceiling has sparkles in it. I feel something between my legs, wetness, put my hand down my pants. Blood. I lie there, looking at the red of my fingers, I don't know what to do. Call Mom. I dial the number, no answer, call again.

"Hi Mom."

"Sweetie, is that you? Where are you?"

"At home, I finally got my period."

"You got it late like your mother, that's wonderful." She sounds busy. "So you're a woman now. I can't talk. I'll send you bras."

I call my friend Daya.

"Finally," she says.

"I don't know what to do," I say.

"I have some stuff. I'll come over."

I wash the blood off my hand, pull circles of toilet paper and put them in my panties. Then I sit on the front steps and wait for Daya. I hope Dad doesn't come home before she gets here.

In the article Dad writes, 'Similar backgrounds, different temperaments. That's what makes a good match.'

"Your father is everything I was looking for in a man," Miriam says when I first meet her at The Bagelry. "The service had me write a list. A week later, your father knocked on the door. I knew he was the man for me. He was all I had written down except for the no money and having a child living with him. It didn't occur to me that a man my age would still have a child at home."

Two months later we move into Miriam's beautiful home a couple blocks from UCSC. The house is very large and surrounded by eucalyptus trees, next to a Jewish cemetery. And here we are, living with one more lady.

My dad has got me tickets for my July trip to Florida. I'll have my sixteenth birthday there. When I was a kid the stewardess would take my hand and give me plastic wings to button on my shirt. Now I'm too old for wings.

Part Two: Adulthood

Garden Parties, Goldilocks and Mozart on the Island

Summer 1987 – Toronto, Algonquin Island

After I graduated high school in Santa Cruz I had a few years to wait for Rilke to finish school. I was seventeen. I didn't want to go to LA without her and I didn't want to stay in Santa Cruz. I would have felt guilty leaving my dad if he wasn't still with Miriam, but he was, and they were in love.

I was homesick for Toronto, for Alex. And Alina, I missed her too. I never wanted her to leave my dad and me. I still called her my stepmom after she left and still wanted her to call me her stepdaughter, like my stepdad did. He always called me his stepdaughter even when my mom and him weren't together anymore.

I went to Toronto. Alina was living on Algonquin Island with Alex, she lived on Dakota, three blocks from our old house on Wyandot where we lived when we were all still a family. I always got sad when I walked down Wyandot.

That summer I worked at a blues bar and a flower store by the lake. I got a part as Goldilocks in the Island play. We had garden night parties with flute players and classical guitars, drank wine out of mason jars: lavender bouquets on the slanted wood table, tea candles lining the pebble path. I slept on the porch and looked at the stars, like I did when I was a little girl on Lasqueti Island and it was just my dad and I. On colder nights I'd tiptoe into Alex or Alina's room and curl up close. Alex would kick me in the night, he was always a restless sleeper but I didn't care. I just wanted to be there.

By winter I had quit my summer job and was working at a fish n' chips stand. The storm windows of the cottage were covered with plastic and the big logs chopped for the wood stove. I shared a bed with Alina. We went to sleep every night listening to Mozart and the wind.

Alina sat by the wood stove on the edge of the chair stitching her Russian dolls. Their wool hair got wilder as the winter went on, and her stitches faster. I got depressed. I ate butter cookies and perogies, wore leather pants, and ate more cookies. I thought about my real mom and Rilke and how I just wanted her to finish school so we could meet in LA and everything would be very good because we would be together.

At night, Alina kept telling me to stop the fidgeting, that she couldn't sleep. By January she said,

"You can't live here anymore."

I wondered if when Alex got to be my age, she would ask him to leave, too. It didn't feel right and I hoped she wouldn't.

I called a friend, Jamie, who lived in the city. He was ten years older than me, a good guy, didn't do drugs or anything like that. French Moroccan, very skinny with chin-length curly black hair. He always wore white and an amethyst hexagon that hung around his neck from a braided leather cord.

"Can I stay with you, just until I find a room somewhere?"

He lived in a yellow house with lots of people and lots of rooms next to a Salvation Army where lines of men stood on

Sundays for soup and bread. No women in those lines. None of us in that house had any money. I had met Jamie when I was working at the fish n' chips place. He liked the way I fried the fish, and he chopped the wood for Alina and me when it got really cold. I had a crush on him but I didn't think he liked me back in that way. There was something asexual about him. Later he told me, "Why else would I have chopped the wood?"

Waiting

January 1988 – Toronto in the City

I ended up renting half the bedroom at Jamie's. Christmas lights separated my side from his. I kept the fish n' chips job and also got a weekend job for Greenpeace canvassing in the snow. A whole crew of us canvassers got in a van and were dropped off in Rosedale, a residential area with fat houses and big snowy lawns. Door to door I'd go with my clipboard and notes on what to say. I got to knocking and hoped that one of these houses had a man who would answer and invite me in for hot chocolate and fall in love with me. He would love me so much, almost as much as my dad loves his poems and my mom her men. Or more.

It got so cold out there. Even though it was for a good cause, I started not thinking about the cause and went to SK's Donuts instead for a bear claw and waited for the time when the van would come get us. When I did knock on doors, because I had to come back with some signatures, I found it real hard to try and get money. I got mixed up about where that money was going when the people in the big houses asked too many questions, kind of like when there were too many specials on the menu when I was trying to waitress. Only when I was waitressing, my feet weren't frozen.

Sometimes, on the crowded streetcar, passing the Ontario Parliament with its white columns out front and ivy growing up towards the windows, I'd think maybe if I dressed up I could get a job answering phones behind that big door. I could be all put together with stockings and my hair pulled back into a bun, sitting at a reception desk with my back straight, all proper. Like my aunt, great-grandma, and grandma when they were lawyers, only I would be a receptionist. I could work nine to five, bring lunch, set the alarm for six every morning, and everything would feel orderly and clean.

Something about the parliament buildings started me thinking about college and how my mom was the only girl in her graduating class in architecture school. And how at twenty-seven my dad taught at Cornell and the Iowa's Writers Program. In high school I'd had good grades and even though I wasn't a cheerleader, didn't drive a new Volkswagen Bug, have a football boyfriend or a tan, I'd joined the Girls' Honor Society.

I started looking into colleges and applied to three. I was most interested in the Theater or English department, but those were competitive majors so on one application I chose Religion, thinking it would be easier to get in. I could change majors later.

One night I came home crying.

"I can't take one more day of frying fish or frozen feet," I told Jamie.

"You say that every night," he said, giving me a kiss and handing me a letter.

By that time we were together. It still felt more like a friendship though. Rarely was he interested in sex. He was all into his health and saving his energy for spiritual work. Like meditating and things like that. Sometimes I thought maybe he was gay or that it had to do with me. That if I was prettier, skinnier, smarter.

I opened the letter, it was from Concordia University in Montreal. I had been accepted into the Religion department and given a small grant for the first semester.

That September Jamie and me took the five-hour train ride to Montreal with three hockey bags and two foam mattresses. It was his idea to bring two beds.

"I've decided to take a one-month vow of celibacy. The yogi's didn't have sex, and I want to connect with you on a deeper level. To feel the universal oneness of the spirit."

I didn't like this celibacy idea, but I didn't see how I could make him sleep in my bed if he didn't want to.

We had found a cheap apartment next to Concordia. The day we moved in, the landlady was standing on the lawn waving to us, her long white hair blowing in all directions.

"You on top floor so is okay," she said as we followed her up the stairs. "Below is after hours for teenagers. Instead of no good business that kids do, for them we make pool hall. You be happy here."

A week later Jamie said, "I need to do something for myself." He wrapped his thin arms around me and tried to swing me off the ground. "You know we're meant to be together, don't you? I really believe that. But last night I felt my soul was trying to tell me something. I was really trying to tune in."

"Is that when you went out for a walk?" I asked.

"I couldn't come up with it so I just thought I'd sleep on it. Bam, woke up and I knew hitchhiking's the plan. I'm going to Vermont and then back again. A couple weeks, three tops."

I took a slight step back from him. He stood there in his dingy white underwear and gray wool socks. His pale, hairy legs looked skinnier to me.

I straightened out the blanket on my bed. "You're so restless."

He ran his fingers through his black, curly hair. "You wanna see if there's any grub below?"

Without looking up I said, "It's for teenagers."

He beat on his chest. "I feel like a teenager. And you are one," he said, pinching my arm. "You know what I wanna get you before I go? A fridge. My girl has gotta have a fridge."

Two days later Jamie and his piece of foam were gone. The night he left, I sat on the cold floor, staring out the window at the gyro stand across the street. The voices from the community center below echoed through the hardwood floors that still needed to be sanded down. The used fridge hummed too loud. A draft came through the curtain-less windows.

The first day of class I arrived at an old brick building with a bronze plaque on the double wooden doors. 'In Jesus We Pray.' Inside was a life-sized sculpture of Jesus hanging from the cross with his eyes open looking at me. I stared back. Then I turned around and walked out. I did not imagine majoring in Religion meant being religious. I never went back.

Somehow, even though I had no talent for drawing or painting, I talked my way into the art department. I showed up to my first class late. I opened the door and a naked man was sitting on a steel stool in the middle of the room, his legs relaxed and spread open.

Easels were set up in a circle, students holding charcoal made broad fast lines across large sheets of paper. I looked at the man in the middle. I was sitting across from the naked man and thought of Jesus on the cross in the religion department.

The teacher had a French accent. "Capture the essence. Feel it in you, close your eyes. *Le beau*."

After the model pulled on trousers and a shirt, the class moved outdoors and we sat under autumn trees with mango- and red-colored leaves.

"Now, the essence of the tree trunk," the teacher said, looking at me with doubt.

At the end of class the teacher looked at my tree trunk. "This tree has the essence of nothing."

That afternoon I bought an easel, charcoal, and watercolors. I went home, ate jam on rye bread, listened to the clarinet players next door, and stared at the blank easel. I had forgotten to buy paper. I already knew I was not going to be an artist. I thought of the young poets coming to my dad for advice. I had no doubt they knew what they were doing and knew how to get the help they needed but here, at eighteen, I had no idea what I was doing.

I spent my time walking through the streets of Montreal. I couldn't handle one more day of pacing around the empty apartment and looking out the window for Jamie. I had no desire to make my place livable. The heat and the phone hadn't been turned on yet.

Cockroaches with a brown metallic sheen appeared every day

when the sun went down. I slept with the lights on so I could trick them into thinking it was still daytime. I spent most of my time walking around the city, especially at night. I wanted to run into Leonard Cohen.

Jamie had sent me three postcards, all saying the same thing, "We are meant to be together. Heading back within the week."

I was fixated on the image of a curvy older woman in a red truck picking him up on a foggy night. If he had stayed I don't think things would have been much better.

My whole life was nothing more than a kind of waiting. Waiting for my mom to come home, even though she never did. She'd sent me a package when I was five, and I'd waited for more. I waited for her letters where she would describe her world in detail, especially the different men in her life. I also waited for my dad—when he went to India to hang out with a swami, or the writers' colonies in upstate New York and New Hampshire. Then there was the time he went to live alone at an art colony in New Mexico. Then Alina left and I watched him wait for her to come home and I waited for him to stop waiting. I waited for this terrible longing in me to go away, and I knew no one was coming back to fix it.

My grant was running out. I became a regular at the gyro stands, went to matinee movies, and walked the streets some more. I looked at women dressed like Audrey Hepburn who sat at the cafés drinking coffee, and I looked at people who passed me in the streets who seemed like they knew exactly where they were going and who they were.

It was a freezing Saturday night. I had been walking along the streets for most of the evening. The snow fell heavy onto the slushy pavement. Happy couples glided past me, holding each other close for warmth. The wind was rubbing my face raw. I wrestled with the folding door of a phone booth until it shut. With my back leaning against the glass I slid to the ground. Huddled there I began to shake, tears streaming down my cheeks, my nose running, eyes blurred. I looked up at the phone. Who could I call? Like a little girl I looked at the big, black handle of the phone. I wanted my mom.

Suddenly there was a hard rap above my head. I turned around and saw a stocky man with a gray mustache wearing oversized galoshes. He motioned to the phone in an urgent manner. I got to my feet and picked up the receiver. The man began pacing in circles around the booth. My heart started to race.

The operator answered, and I gave her the number I memorized a long time ago. I listened to the static.

"A collect call from," the operator said.

My teeth began chattering. I said my name.

"Do you accept the charges?"

"Yes," my mom said. "Honey?"

"Hi," I said.

"I was just thinking of you."

"You were?"

"Just today I showed your picture to a nice man. He said you look just like me."

"Everyone says I look like Dad."

"You got the best of both of us," she said.

"My hair is longer now."

"You have your mom's hair. We have beautiful Jewish hair."

I looked down at my damp boots. "What were you doing before I called?"

"In bed, reading a great article in *The New Yorker*. I'll send it to you."

"It's really cold here."

"I'll send you a heating blanket right away," she said. "We don't like the cold, do we? Do you know how proud your mom is of you?"

What could she be proud of?

"I had a guy and he left," I said.

"We girls don't lose the men we adore. I'm sure you didn't want him anyway. I have a great guy now who mows the lawn."

Mom always had at least two men in her life.

"The grass looks good?"

There was still static on the line.

"Is that my phone?" she asked.

"I'm at a payphone."

Turning around, I looked at the stocky man. His hands were in his pockets; he was staring up at the snowy sky. I started crying.

"You need to come home and be with your mother," she said.

"I have this fridge. Jamie got it for me."

"Fridge? Fuck the fridge. I'm putting a ticket in the mail first thing tomorrow morning."

I knew Rilke and my stepdad wouldn't be there. They were in Iowa, where my stepdad grew up. Rilke had started to get into trouble in eighth grade stealing and not going to school and Paul thought Florida was part of the problem and it was. She did better in Iowa.

I wasn't sure I wanted to go without her there, but I didn't want to stay in Montreal anymore and maybe it would be different, being with my mom alone. I hung up the phone and walked out of the booth. My body felt less numb. The man was still there.

"It's so windy," he said, unfolding a scrap piece of paper.

I looked at him and as I walked home I wondered who he was going to call.

My Mother's Men

On the plane ride to Florida, I thought about my mom. Like how smart she was to be the only girl in the architecture program at Michigan, how beautiful she was, how she said no to being in *Playboy* when they were scouting college girls on campus, and how she wasn't interested in any boys in high school.

"I just concentrated on my studies," she had told me.

Then I started thinking about when was it that she started to have so many men, and I pretty much didn't stop thinking about them until the plane landed. She had lots of them, always lined up just in case. Every summer when I went to visit there was a new one. Sometimes they moved in but then they would move out pretty fast. Most of the time she just went to their house.

Like Marco, I remember the day she told Rilke and me about him. She was really late picking us up from Ellen Swope Dance class.

"I met Marco," she said. "A lifeguard on Lido Beach, all six-two of him, dark, Italian. I had on my yellow bikini. The best sex I ever had. He's twenty-three."

Mom was forty.

A couple of years later he was all gray, but he was still around. He smoked pot, watched cartoons, and sat in his lifeguard station looking through binoculars, sometimes saving lives. He watched the women in bikinis lying on their rainbow-colored towels in the white Florida sand all around his tower. It must have been about five years later when my mom stopped taking us to Lido Beach. We went to Siesta Key instead. Lido had cherry slushes and we missed the slushes. We didn't miss Marco.

Sometimes Mom would wash her thick blonde hair at 3 p.m., lying on her bed waiting for Marco to call. Sometimes he wouldn't, not for months. Rilke and I called him Weeds because he always came back.

Some days, when Mom dropped Rilke and me off at Ellen Swope Dance where we took tap, ballet, and jazz, she'd drive past Marco's bungalow on the way.

Sometimes she'd stop and tell us, "You two wait in the car."

One time we ran up to the window and heard them behind the screen.

"I don't even have my own drawer here," she told him. "I don't want your other girls parking in front of your house when they spend the night. You tell them to park on the side streets and not to put kiss notes on the windshield of the truck I bought you."

When Mom picked us up from dance that day she said, "He moved his socks for me and now I have my own drawer."

Mom herself wasn't devoted to one person.

"Girls, you can't look to one man for everything."

There was Wayne, the alcoholic telephone-pole worker. Short, thin, hardly spoke.

"He has good teeth," my mom said.

Most of the boarders at our house were missing teeth. She'd rent them rooms. She only slept with men who had good teeth. Lobster smelled like fish. Glenn, aka Loose Balls, wore gray nylon shorts, and when he sat down you could see a red squashed ball. Loose Balls took Rilke and me to the mall one day and bought us each a pair of bell-bottom jeans.

Then mom took us for a checkup at the red-cheeked dentist, Chuck. He stuck his fat hands in our mouths and looked around. We put him on the bad list next to Weeds. My mom was with Pool Man the night before he drowned. Tall, handsome, good teeth. I pictured him face-down in that pool with his good legs and arms all brown, just floating there. Then there was Juicy, who rode elephants at Ringling Circus, and Don, wearing brown leather cutoff gloves, driving his yellow Trans Am.

One night, Mom pulled out the leather journal she kept under the mattress.

"Last year I slept with a hundred men." She looked through the pages. "Two of them baseball players. Training season can be tough. They were so delighted to have me in the middle of practice. The two of them arrived in their White Sox uniforms. That was a good year."

Frank started off as a boarder and then moved into Mom's bed. Wore acid-washed jeans and tanks loose under his armpit. He had red, muscled arms and pimples on his shoulders. He paced around in workman boots, laces untied. When he moved into Mom's bed, Rilke and I didn't like hearing them have sex, but he never looked at us creepy, and he left root beer in the fridge for us next to mom's red zinger tea and frosted sheer nail polish where eggs should have been.

She didn't like food in the fridge. Didn't like food.

"Little Grandma is five feet six and has never weighed more than a hundred and two pounds," she told us. "And you know your grandpa, he didn't like to operate on fat people. He was such a good surgeon, you know."

One day Mom chased Frank around the house with a needle thing like a shot. Maybe he was chasing her, it was all fast. She had that needle and poked him and he fell and she ran and came back with rope. Tied his feet and hands, called the cops. When Rilke and I heard the sirens, we got on our bikes and rode to Gulf Gate Mall. Paid two dollars for a matinee of a French movie we didn't want to see and when we came back, Frank was gone and Mom was painting tee shirts, all spread out on the back lawn. She had on a sky-blue men's button-down. Her legs and feet were bare.

"Let's go for raisin bagels in the morning, girls."

And then there was Terry, the masseuse with a criminal record for molesting women. I can't imagine going to prison in Florida. Too hot.

Mom had another man that went to prison, Helmet Head. His real name was Roy. He was a tall, hairy sculptor who rented out our garage as a work studio. He made monumental fish. I remember that day. The day Roy left. He had bought me and Rilke a hammock, stringing it just high enough between two lemon trees so we could see his fish through the garage window. Roy didn't live with us, but it felt like he did.

Every morning, we'd been waking up to the crunch of gravel as he pulled into the driveway on his black motorcycle. There was a chipped yellow stripe on the gas tank. He'd bring a paper bag lunch with him: two crunchy peanut-butter-and-banana sandwiches on rye, a dill pickle, and half a dozen gingersnaps. But he always ate it somewhere else. I made him a sunny-side-up egg sandwich once, his favorite. He asked if I could pack it up for him.

"He's got a lunchtime lover," my mom said. I couldn't tell if she was jealous or not.

It was late afternoon. The air was still and humid, smelling of sulfur from the running hose hooked up to the well. Smoky clouds drifted over the white ones. Rilke and I were lying in the hammock with our legs extended toward the sky. I remember my big toe was a deep purplish red. I had stubbed it earlier. I wiped the sweat off my upper lip. Lightning sliced the clouds. We waited for thunder. Then we heard an engine coming down the street, fast. Roy accelerated onto the sidewalk, across the lawn, behind the house. I don't know why, but we froze in the netting under the trees. Roy started walking towards us. His high forehead and lined cheeks looked pale, moist. A damp brown paper bag was tucked under his armpit. Sirens. Mom ran outside. Six cop cars surrounded the house.

Roy was Helmet Head. At the time anyone south of Gainesville knew about Helmet Head, the lunchtime robber. He'd target small-town Florida banks on his motorcycle. But he never pulled the trigger on his gun, and he never took off his helmet. Thirty-nine banks in two years.

I couldn't believe it. There was nothing I knew that had been mean or menacing about him. All I ever saw him do was sculpt his fish. He never said much, but when he did talk it was all about his two kids.

"My ex-lady," he had said. "She has them during the week and I take em' on the weekends. Come Wednesday, I miss them something terrible."

Sometimes they had come with him to sculpt. Rilke and me would peek in the window and see all three of them with oversized plastic safety goggles on as Helmet Head showed them how to torch the bronze. Maybe he became a lunchtime robber to support his kids. I had always wondered how he made his money.

I even missed Roy a bit when he was taken away. In the beginning, Mom would ask Rilke and me if we wanted to go with her to see Roy on visiting day. I didn't like the idea of going to prison at all. Neither did Rilke, so we never did. Besides

Mom would be gone whole days waiting in line with all the other women to see their men. Not that Mom and Roy ever made it known they had a thing, but I got a pretty good feeling he was another of her men.

Watching Mom and all her men, I wanted no part of growing up to be a woman who jumped from man to man, and definitely not being with a man who ever went to prison.

Visiting Prison with Frank

December 1988 – Florida

"Welcome to the Sunshine State," the stewardess announced. She had on orange lipstick that blended in with her tan. "We're pleased to inform you it's a clear eighty-five-degree day with no expected showers."

I was seated in the back of the plane and one of the last to get off. As I waited I took out a compact hand mirror and reapplied my eyeliner and blackberry lipstick. Then I remembered my mom didn't like dark lipstick. With the back of my hand I tried to wipe it off. I made sure there was no sleepy crust in my eyes and that my zipper was up on my baggy black pants.

I walked off the plane into the sunlight. It glared into my eyes as I made my way down the stairs. My hand tightened around the railing and I stopped.

I remembered the excitement I had felt whenever I was on my way to Florida. A squat, bald man with a square face in front of me held out his arms as he ran towards a woman with a big head of blonde hair. I wiped off the sweat that was forming on my upper lip.

A tall beefy man wearing a loose gray tank top caught my eye. It was Frank the thug, and he was looking at me. He reached for his sunglasses that were propped on his forehead and put them on. Then as if in slow motion he put one heavy foot in front of the other and walked towards me. He kept one hand behind his back. The crowd had thinned out quick. He walked right up to me. I felt my throat tighten and my eyes water up as I scanned behind him for my mom.

"Your mom really wanted to make it. We're meeting her at a motel," he said, extending a white rose from the hand that was behind his back. "She wanted me to give you this."

She had remembered white roses were my favorite. We got my hockey bag and jumped in his car.

"It's good to see you again. You remember last time, it didn't end so well but you know, your mom's a good gal. I needed a room again and she rented me one. I been staying with her 'bout five months now." He lit a cigarette and rolled down the window. "You hungry?" he asked.

"No." I looked out the window at the tall palm trees as we got on the interstate. I never flew directly to Mom's in Sarasota because it was cheaper not to. The sleeve holes on his tank top were extra low. I could see his chest and it looked kind of puffy and his nipples seemed red and hard. I'd never seen a man with a chest like that before.

"I don't like to drive fast so it'll take us 'bout an hour." He turned on the radio. Santana was playing.

"Want me to roll up the window?" he asked.

"It's okay." The hot air and cigarette smoke blew in my face.

Hanging from the rearview mirror was a fluorescent clock in the shape of an orange. I stared at the flat road ahead. Frank made noise when he breathed. I looked at the pimples on his big sunburnt arm. "How old are you?" I asked.

"Guess."

"Forty-five?"

"You sure answered that fast." He lit his fifth cigarette. He took a long drag on it and turned towards me. He held in his smoke as he stared into my eyes. I stared back at him trying not to blink. But it was hard because the wind was still blowing in my face. He finally turned the other way and exhaled, letting the smoke glide out of his chapped mouth. It seemed to blow right into his eyes. They were blue with red veins. One of my dad's women, she had eyes like that.

I looked away from Frank. I started to feel the humidity even more. My armpits and inner thighs felt sticky. He turned up the music.

"Maybe you're younger than forty-five," I said. "You have some pimples like me."

"You don't have pimples."

He turned off the four-lane highway. I was glad because I had to pee bad. We passed Alligator Alley and went down a narrow road for a few miles.

Frank pulled into an old yellow motel. "We're meeting your mom here."

There were many cars out front. The paint was chipping off and the roof was missing tiles. The grass was crowded with plastic pink flamingos. A boy of about four with white-blonde hair was trying to fix a loose chain on his dirt bike. Next to him was a three-foot-high vinyl blow-up pool in the shape of a duck. A mother in a red- and orange-polka-dot bikini sat in it, breast-feeding her baby.

I turned to Frank. "She's here?"

"Soon. You can clean up and rest a bit," he said as we got out of the car.

"Where is she?"

"She's visiting a friend of ours up the road some. We're gonna spend the night here and head home in the morning." He leaned down to pick up a baby bottle, half full of chocolate milk.

I knew there was a prison up the road and I assumed she was visiting Helmet Head. It seemed strange to me that Frank knew Helmet Head and even more so that they were friends, but I didn't say anything.

A naked little boy ran up to me. "Will you be my girlfriend?" He squirted me with a footlong plastic gun. I shot him with my forefinger. He dropped at my feet. I looked down. He was breathing hard, his belly rising and falling. The corners of his mouth were stained with grape juice.

I stopped for a moment. My eyes glazed over as I stared at one of the fallen flamingos. "Don't you want to visit your friend, too?" I asked Frank.

"Listen," he said. "Hear the crickets?"

It sounded like a forest of them.

"I saw him recently. Your mom doesn't make it down here much." He opened the screen door for me as we entered the motel. There was no air-conditioning but a fan sat on the counter.

A heavy woman in a white halter-top sat watching TV. "You folks got reservations?" she asked without looking at us. "Cause if you don't I can tell you now, there ain't an empty bed for miles."

Frank set the bottle on the counter. Then he walked over to fix the coat-hanger antenna on the TV.

"Frank. Why didn't you speak up? Always creeping up on me like that."

He leaned over to kiss her on the cheek.

She blushed.

"You got two rooms?" Frank asked.

"Two, I ain't got one, you know what it's like on holidays. Women gotta see their men inside."

She turned around and eyed me for a moment, standing with her hands on her hips. "But for you," she swatted Frank on the butt, "I'll give you one room and bring a cot for the princess."

Frank and I were in the shadowy room alone. He went to the bathroom and splashed water on his face. There was no door on it.

"I'm going out for a cigarette," he said.

I sat on the edge of the bed.

He walked over to me, cocked his head to one side, then gently took his callused hand and ruffled the top of my head.

Turning away he said, "Your mom's gonna be happy to see you. I got root beer at home in the fridge for you." He closed the door behind himself.

The room smelled like mildew and mothballs. An air-conditioner was installed in the window, I turned it on, it rattled. I leaned back on the bed and closed my eyes. I probably should have been more surprised that Mom was visiting one of her men in prison but I wasn't. I had always liked watching prison movies. I pictured her standing in the visiting line with other women, the hours she had to wait in the heat, the money she put down on the books for his cigarettes and extra food, and the look on her face when she sat down and picked up the phone and talked to him through the thick glass until the buzzer went off.

Some kid was crying outside my window. My eyes were still shut. Maybe they'd been closed for too long, but I still didn't want to open them. The whole room felt like it was swirling.

The Pink Flamingo

It was the first time being with my mom without Rilke and my stepdad there, and I had imagined maybe being one-on-one with her I'd get to know her more. I lasted three months. She took me to Ross and bought me capri pants and we ate raisin bagels with butter. But not too much butter, I didn't want to gain the few pounds I had lost since I had been there.

"You just need to eat watermelon for three days," she told me the first day I was there. "You have a beautiful body honey."

I made myself do it for five, a watermelon a day. During that time my mom had no money. There was always no money but this time she really had no money. I never asked her how she was able to send me a ticket to Florida. We went to Happy Hour at The Quay by the water. With an order of one drink we got to watch the red orange Florida sunset and eat free sesame crackers with jack cheese, salami, and grapes.

"One iced tea," my mom would say to the bartender.

Sometimes she ordered a Tab with lime and when the bartender was cute, she'd order one for each of us. I was glad she did because I was embarrassed when we shared one. I liked those nights with my mom, driving with her in her old steel blue Mercedes that a whole lot of days didn't start.

But living with her in her old Spanish house, we weren't really alone. She still had rented rooms to men. Frank wasn't sharing a bed with her this time and was sleeping in Rilke's old room upstairs with her Whitney Houston poster still on the wall and steroid needles under the bed. I know because one day when he was gone I went in there and looked around. Lobsterman, who had been living there last time I visited, still rented a room on the ground floor, and the butcher from Morton's Market lived in the back house.

Some night's Mom went to see Marco, her lifeguard lover, and I was alone with these men. I felt scared and I didn't want to be there but I didn't know where to go. I wanted my mom to come home. One night when she was gone, Lobsterman came back from a day of fishing and he had a party and the whole house smelled like fish. I locked myself in Mom's big room and stared out the old Spanish windows at the tops of the palm trees and the neighbor's tiled roof. I listened for crickets, like I did every night. They kept me company but that night I didn't hear them and I closed my eyes and tried extra hard to hear but I only heard Lobsterman's friends.

I unlocked the door, ran to the top of the stairs and screamed, "Shut up, shut up!"

I worked at The Pink Flamingo, a wine bar on Main Street. I rode my beach cruiser that one of Mom's men let me borrow. The Flamingo was more known for its pumpkin bread than the wine. Everyone who went got the pumpkin bread.

One night, a man walked in, six-foot-four with a strong jaw

and green eyes. Cole. He was the most handsome man I'd ever seen and he didn't stop staring at me and I wished I looked better. I was wearing a blousy skirt that made me feel fat. He was older, forty-one. I was almost nineteen.

I liked that he was older. I felt protected and thought people would think that I must be a smart girl if a man his age liked me. He picked me up at my mom's to take me to dinner, I didn't know how to drive yet. I had never had a man do that before. When my bicycle tire popped he loaded it in the trunk and took it to the bike store.

"That's what boyfriends do," he said.

I didn't even know he considered me his girlfriend, I felt special but I was also scared of my feelings for him and that maybe I was just another girl to him. Sometimes I told him I was busy on a Saturday night when he wanted to take me out because I wanted him to miss me and like me more.

Cole lived in Miami and was in Sarasota putting together the Ringling College film department. Every weekend he made the five-hour drive down Alligator Alley to go back home. When we met he started to go every other weekend. Sometimes I went with him. I think it was on one of those drives that I fell in love. I just wanted to be near him and he wanted to be near me.

I started thinking about college again. I had two more years until Rilke graduated. There was a theater program in Miami that had a good reputation but I didn't think I could get in. Anna Alexander, my summer theater camp teacher who drove the yellow VW Bug and wore Cherries In The Snow lipstick, she was taking me to Denny's once a week for a chocolate malt. We sat in the same red vinyl booth every Friday.

"I will help you with your application," she said. "We will choose a Shakespeare and a contemporary monologue for your audition."

I didn't know why she would do that. Spend her time on me. I wondered that as a kid too when Rilke and me would spend the night with her and read Anne Frank.

The night I got the letter in the mail there was thunder and lightning and I came home from the Flamingo on my beach cruiser all wet and there were no lights on in the house. I didn't even wait to go inside to open the letter. I had been accepted.

I had three months before the college semester started and I needed to come up with tuition. I didn't want to live in the house with the smell of fish, Lobsterman, the Butcher or Frank any more, and when a friend called and told me that she was filming a show with Oprah in Chicago for the summer and that I could come and stay with her, that's what I did. Cole didn't want me to go and I knew it would be hard being away from him but then he could really miss me and I wouldn't come across as a needy woman. I was also scared of really getting to know him and him to know me and if I left first he couldn't leave me. I also knew I would miss having bagels and sharing a Tab at the quay while watching the sunset with my mom, but I had to go.

Blow-Up Girls

When I arrived in Chicago, the film my friend had a part in had put her up in a twenty-third-floor apartment on State Street near the Water Tower. It came furnished with hotel lamps, beige curtains, crystal chandeliers, white carpet, and a sunken living room that I slept in.

We ate Cobb salads five nights a week in a diner with brown vinyl booths below the high rise. The other two nights we ate Chicago burgers and drank laxative Lacie Le Beau tea. We'd wake up with stomachaches in the night and swear no more burgers or Lacie. We rented movies and went to our first peep show next to the video store, across the street from Mickey's Blues. Blow-up dolls in the window with blonde hair and checkered mini-skirts in knee-highs, brunettes with cherry red lips and black vinyl thigh-high boots. We walked by the blow-up girls every night that we rented a movie. Us staring at them, them staring at us. Waiting to be bought. The dolls made us feel fat and sad.

I got a job at 24 Hour Fitness. The 5 a.m. shift checking people in. I stood there in the uniform of white nylon shirt and shiny blue spandex leggings. Lasted three days. On the last day I went home at lunch, made a tuna sandwich, and never went back. I spread the *Chicago Tribune* out on the table and turned to the classified job section. Hostess at pizzeria, typist at law firm, caregiver.

I thought of my first job, back when I was nine, cleaning houses on Algonquin Island. A neighbor and his navy blue Hanes underwear on the floor, folding and putting them in his drawer, cleaning his sink and toilet with Ajax, finding quarters and putting them in my pockets.

I turned the page to the adult classified section. *Escorts Wanted – Earn three hundred dollars an hour.* I got up and opened another can of tuna. I wondered what that would be like, to be an escort. I had already been with men I didn't want to be with for no money. Only a couple, but that was enough. When it happened something in me froze. I wanted to say no but I couldn't, I didn't feel like I had a choice. If I were an escort, it would be my choice. Maybe I could do it, just for a couple months and then that's it, get some money together for tuition and rent and stop.

I wondered how other girls made their money. The ones that didn't have parents that gave it to them while they were building their lives. They must have worked forty, sixty hours a week waitressing in the summer before college, maybe even two jobs. Cocktail waitressing at night, and during the day standing at the front desk at 24 Hour Fitness in spandex checking people in like I had done for three days.

I couldn't waitress. I was no good at it. And the spandex job paid eight dollars an hour. Maybe the girls who waitressed hadn't met any men in brown cars or had a guy babysitter. Maybe if there never was a brown car man or babysitter I never would have looked at the adult classified section.

I threw the second can of tuna out and picked up the phone.

That Saturday I took the L train to the South Side, met a man at a deep-dish pizza diner.

"The girls call me Mr. Sam," he said. He was a thin man, bald with eyebrows that met in the middle. "Order whatever you like, but I'll tell you they have a mean garlic bread."

"Coffee would be good," I said.

The waitress walked over.

"Coffee for the little lady," he told her. "And bring us a basket of that fine garlic bread."

I didn't know what to say, and Mr. Sam, he just kinda talked like he had known me a while. He talked with his wrists, lots of gestures.

"No need to explain nothing," he said. "And I ain't gonna ask you a trail of questions. I got the feeling you need to make a little money and you got not a thing to worry over."

After coffee and garlic bread we walked across the street to his office/apartment. There was a velour zebra on the wall. Three girls sat on a jungle-green fake leather couch underneath the zebra with their legs crossed, eating baloney sandwiches. Another one sat on the floor filing her nails. They didn't acknowledge us as we walked in. I followed Mr. Sam to the back office.

"All I need is an ID and for you to undress," he said.

I undressed and stood there, pale and nervous. Mr. Sam leaned back in his swivel chair behind his desk, motioned for me to turn around.

"Looking good, no visible scars, no tats. I think I can do something with you."

Two nights later I was sitting on the jungle couch with the

other girls eating baloney sandwiches on whole wheat with yellow mustard.

What I remember most about the first man was his penis smelling like baby powder and the driver waiting outside not saying a word before or after. I wondered if he had a book while he waited for me.

"Act like you've been at this a while," Mr. Sam had said. "He wants a young blonde who knows what she's doing."

I tripped on a rug in the hotel lobby. My forehead and jaw felt tight as I entered the man's room. He was maybe fifty, bald, a paunch but not a big one. He handed me an envelope before walking towards the bed and lying down with his hands clasped behind his head. I just stood next to the bed in my black mini dress and heels. Kinda frozen, like.

I thought about Mr. Sam telling me to act like I had done this before. That made me more nervous. I felt like I was supposed to make a move, ask him to unclasp my bra, lick my lips as I loosened his belt buckle. My heart was racing, I tried to make a move, to speak, but I couldn't. What was I doing? I wanted him to tell me what to do. I wanted it to be over.

"You're new, aren't you?" he asked.

I didn't answer but my hand moved and I was relieved. This hand that didn't feel like my hand sliding the dress over my head. I imagined one of the girls on the jungle couch, the bleached blonde with high cheekbones that she accentuated with a foundation shimmer, the one who also did porn.

I heard the words come out of my mouth: "Take off your pants."

This voice that didn't sound like mine. Envisioning this girl, picturing what she would do in a porn, I tried to pretend I was her. That I was playing a part. I began to touch myself. The man's small hairless dick grew hard.

"I want to see you stroke it," I said.

He did. I watched his hand slide up and down, up and down, but not in a steady rhythm. More like fast, fast then jerky. I got on all floors and looked behind at him.

"I want to feel you in me," I said.

Behind. Yes, better than being on top of him or his weight on me. I didn't have to see his face, his expressions. I could hardly feel his dick, but he was going fast, hands planted firmly on my hips, in and out. I felt like I was holding my breath as I waited for it to be over.

The porno girl, I pictured her moaning, and as I did I felt myself float above, as if she had replaced me and was doing 'the work' while I watched. I moaned and the man, he came. It was over and I left, I felt I could breathe again. Nothing about it felt real. I was detached, like I was watching myself play a part in a movie going through the motions but I wasn't a good actress. (He never called for me again and I was relieved. I felt embarrassed with him. Embarrassed that he knew I had no experience. Similar to how I felt with my first boyfriend when I tried to pretend I knew what I was doing.)

That first night, I went home and ate air popcorn, spraying I Can't Believe It's Not Butter on the kernels in the dark. The next night I took the L train to work and told myself I could do it, I'd do better than the first night. I wouldn't be so stiff.

I didn't do better. A redheaded man with freckles, a kind, doughy-looking face wanted me to talk dirty and I can't explain but I felt like I was in a thick fog and forgot all about the porno girl and how she had helped me the first time. I went blank and couldn't get the words out so we ate cinnamon twists together and he told me I should go with a more high-class service.

"You have the looks," he said. "Even if you can't talk dirty."

He gave me money without having sex, and a donut for the driver on the way home. I was grateful he had been a nice man. I imagined he called for another girl, maybe a repeat to make sure he got one who could tell him he was a bad boy and deserved a spanking.

The next guy was young and thin with curly brown hair pulled back in a ponytail. He had an apartment full of hardback books and sketches of ballerinas framed in chipped windowpanes without the glass. He seemed sad. He was different. If we didn't meet the way we did maybe, I don't know, he said he liked me. I liked him and his books on the stairs leading up to his bedroom, Bukowski and *Leaves of Grass* with Whitman on the cover under a tree.

"Why can't I just meet a girl like you?" he asked.

He took my hand and led me to his bedroom and started kissing me. I felt comfortable with him. Maybe it was the familiarity of his surroundings, the books, the sketches. I was surprised that I liked his lips against mine, the feeling of closeness. I didn't mind him on top of me. I wanted all the men to be like him or versions of him. Not unattractive, gentle. But they weren't. I left that night feeling lonely. An aching that I didn't like, a longing to find comfort in another, but who?

During the day I walked a mile down State Street to Fitness World, took an aerobics class in a room full of magenta and hot-pink spandex. Walked back down State Street past the billboards for United Colors of Benetton, wedding dress shops, boutiques and home to an iceberg salad with no-oil tuna and low-fat ranch dressing.

At night I walked down the steps into the subway station. A man with a rainbow knitted hat played the flute, eyes closed, his whole body moving, real smooth like. Coins and dollars in his open flute case. Tonight I told myself, I just know I'll make some good money. Flute man's got these black work boots on, laces untied; his feet look too big for his body. I wondered what he did during the day with those feet that didn't match his graceful body.

The subway reminded me of being a kid in Toronto. The winter cold, walking down into the subway, croissants baked at this one stop, Union Station. Those doors would open and that warm smell would come in with the wind. I had my toe shoes and pink ballet tights in my knapsack and my hair in a bun, all knotted up with bobby pins. Off to ballet class I would go, five nights a week and here I was, ten years later, dressed in a black tube-top dress, teased hair and red ninety-nine-cent Wet N' Wild lips, on my way to sit with other girls on a fake leather couch under a velvet framed picture. All of us waiting for a man to call, hoping and not hoping we would fit the description. We waited and ate more baloney sandwiches. Some nights, when I felt fat and that I needed to lose five pounds, I'd chew a wad of bubble gum instead.

Four hours later I was eating pizza with an Indian man at a Ramada Inn. He had a beautiful Indian accent. I thought of my dad and the sari he bought for me when he went to India. The gold-threaded sari that I wrapped myself in when the bad babysitter told me to get naked. I hadn't thought of the babysitter in so long and the memory of him punched me in the stomach.

I could hardly get the words out.

"May I use your restroom?" I asked the Indian man.

I sat on the lid of the toilet and told myself to calm down, take three breaths. I squeezed my eyes shut as if that would make the memory go away. And it did or at least I pretended to myself it did. I pushed the memory and any feelings I had about it deep down within myself like I had done all my life.

We sat cross-legged on the brown carpet which had navy-blue paisleys on it. I kept staring at it, the paisleys reminded me of snails. I wanted to be a snail, to curl up into myself, small. So small. There was a faint smell of cigarettes that hovered above the aroma of cheese. I picked the warm pieces of pineapple off my slice of pizza.

"You're beautiful," he said.

After pizza he turned off all the lights except the lamp on the nightstand next to a Bible. I had stayed at hotels before that had Bibles by the bed but they had been kept in a drawer. I wondered if this man had taken it out and was reading it. The whole time I kept thinking about the black Bible. Why? I had no good or bad association with it. Maybe it was just something concrete in the room to concentrate on while this man did his thing or maybe it was just something to think about as I waited for it to be over. Always, I couldn't wait for it to end as soon as it started.

Porn girl. She wore a gold cross. I wondered what her up-bringing was like. Was she raised reading the Bible, going to church and having to go to confession? That would be terrible, to feel like I'd be going to hell for my sins. I already felt bad. I was aware of that and in a way that made it worse. Why, if I knew what I was doing didn't make me feel good, did I keep doing it? I tried not to think about that. Anytime I did I pushed it away and with that I pushed any sense of myself further away too. Somewhere far off, floating above as if a witness to my own life.

The man turned his back to me as he undressed before pulling back the polyester bedspread and getting under the covers. I did the same. He turned the light off. The room was so dark, not a stream of light coming in. It scared me. His small hands caressed my breasts, he lowered his head and started sucking on my nipples, then rolled on top of me and kissed my neck. I felt a shiver go up my spine but not a good kind of shiver. I placed my hand on his dick and guided him in. I was expecting him to be small even though I knew just because a man was short didn't mean he had a short skinny dick. The sex was ordinary and that was good because it made the dark less scary. But he lasted too long and he got sweaty and I didn't want his sweat on me. It felt too intimate which didn't make any sense since here I was having sex with him.

"I would very much like to have the pizza with you again next Friday," he said.

I didn't mind the thought of seeing him again. Compared to other men he was okay.

I went home, ate dark chocolate with raisins and walnuts, and wondered if the Indian had a wife, and if his name was really Mike.

"You don't look like a Betty," he had said.

"My real name is Alina," I lied. "I never tell people."

I wonder why I used my stepmother's name. It sounded real. I think he believed me.

Another man in a high-rise had short legs and a long torso and women's lingerie all spread out on his couch.

"Fulfill my desire," he said, sitting back in a brown leather La-Z-Boy chair. "Let me watch you model the lingerie."

I imagined other women slipping their legs into the lavender lacy things as I unzipped my black pencil skirt, back facing him. All the items were lacy and 80s-looking. I thought about what aerobics class to take tomorrow and what the driver outside who was waiting for me was doing.

Lingerie Man didn't take his clothes off and never stood up from the La-Z-Boy. He unzipped his pants and took out his dick. "Sit on it," he said.

I didn't like this man. The way he leaned back in that leather chair with his legs spread apart. He had a cocky look on his face.

As I rotated my hips round and round, my bracelets rang against each other almost as if in rhythm to my movements. I concentrated on the gentle *clang, clang* as my thighs began to throb. Later, after I left I continued to hear the sound of my bracelets and feel the throbbing of my thighs.

The young one in an empty high-rise. A bed, a digital red blinking alarm clock next to his suit on the floor. I remember feeling a stabbing sensation in my stomach as he pounded away.

"That's it, first base," he grunted.

I didn't know what he was talking about.

"Second, that's right. Hit a home run, hit it," he continued.

Baseball? I didn't know what to think but I wanted to be gone, the stabbing pain in my belly, the baseball. I stared at the digital clock. 12:01 a.m., 12:02. He was in a rush and his hands were clammy and his cologne too strong. I didn't think I was his type. I was insecure. I wished this man was the Indian with the pizza. I was more comfortable with the men from somewhere else, another country, less talking and I liked that they got on a plane and flew away. By 12:08 he hit a home run and it was over, I was in the elevator going down.

The last Chicago man was the Saudi Arabian, and he gave me two thousand to stop. I couldn't believe it, I didn't even kiss him. Why me? I wondered if that ever happened to any of Sam's girls before. I hoped not, I wanted to be the only one, to be special. Maybe it made him feel good about himself, like he was 'saving' some girl. Saving me. Or he had a daughter and there was something about me that reminded him of her. I never could make any sense of it.

I had been instructed to meet him in the lounge of a fancy downtown hotel. He wore a strong cologne that made my nose twitch and had bushy eyebrows that arched way up in the middle with dense black lashes. His eyebrows gave him a distinct sharp look but his eyes were gentle. He studied me closely, not saying anything for a couple minutes.

"Why a girl like you, so soft," he said in a low voice, "No kind of work for you."

I touched the heart-shaped pendant around my neck. "I need to make money for college."

Twisting the corners of his black mustache he looked deep in thought. We left the bar, he was carrying a dark burgundy briefcase with gold clasps. I wondered what was in it and why he brought it with him.

Sitting in his fat silver car he set the briefcase between us, "You're not like the other girls."

I didn't know what he meant by that. He drove towards the lake and parked outside a tall, mirrored building.

"I be right back," he said. "I lock the doors."

I turned around and watched the man enter the building. It was just me sitting there in the passenger seat with the lingering scent of his heavy cologne and that briefcase set next to me. I opened it and there was lots of money. I touched the crisp bills and wanted to take some of it but I didn't. I closed it. I had an image of him watching me with a pair of binoculars through one of the mirrored windows. Why did he leave it there, trusting me with it? He came back, opened it up, and gave me two thousand to stop. I told him I would and I did stop. For a while.

Sleeping with the different men for two months, most weren't that bad. They were nice men and nobody made me do anything I didn't want to do. Like the one that wanted me to talk dirty and even though I couldn't he paid me and then we ate donuts. Or the one I actually liked for real who had ballet pictures framed on his walls, lots of books piled on the staircase and talked about Whitman and Zola before taking my hand and leading me to his bedroom.

With most of the men I had sex with, I went somewhere else. I imagined laying in tall grass in a meadow with dandelions or walking down the aisle at the grocery store and all the different food and the rows of cereal boxes, all the choices and how much I loved cereal and how when I got home that night I'd have some but first I'd have to stop at the store to buy it. Maybe the driver who made me feel safe waiting outside until I was done would take me to the store after.

Sometimes I couldn't make my thoughts go someplace else like when I was with the overweight man who smelled of baby powder. The powder kept bringing me back to him lying on top of me and it made me think of being six with the pale man in the brown car. But soon enough it was over and later I just put him and all the other men out of my head.

Ever since I had seen a movie in eighth grade, *Belle De Jour*, call girls intrigued me. It was about a prostitute. A sophisticated, French beauty that is married. I thought about that movie a lot. In the end it is ambiguous whether it was a dream or not. A part of me felt like I was in a dream. It wouldn't be until years later that I would wake up.

Love with the Older Man
Fall 1989 – Miami

The plan when I got to Miami was to stay with Cole until I found a place on South Beach.

"You will meet some young guy if you live near the beach," he said after I started looking in the paper for singles to rent.

He had a beautiful home that he rented in Coral Gables near the university, and he wanted me to live with him. He was a real bachelor when I met him. Never married, no kids and went to strip clubs a lot. He had dated a beautiful Swedish stripper. I had never been in a strip club before. I wanted to know what that was like. He had lots of women. I know because I saw a list in his office, I found postcards too.

"To my number one hard on Valentine's Day," one said with a red kiss mark and an XOXO. The postcard had a picture of a naked Spanish girl walking out of the ocean. I never got those words or the postcard girl or the beautiful Swedish girl out of my head.

I moved in. Every day at 7 a.m. I rode my bicycle down the streets lined with banyan trees to the tram. Theater School was a long day between acting classes, rehearsals for plays, and required academic courses. I got a part-time job at a boutique in a gym selling spandex magenta short shorts and aqua and pink g-string leotards. It was the late 80s and it was Florida. I had a pair of every color and always took a place at the head of the aerobics class.

From the very beginning I told Cole that I would be going to LA.

"To be with Rilke and to act," I said.

I told him that a lot, and I don't think he believed me. I think Rilke started not to believe me too. Sometimes I wasn't sure I could leave either, since I was in love, and it scared me to think that, but it scared me more to think I would stay.

I spent two years in the theater program and was cast in a few plays and a musical too. I can't sing but I got the part of the lead. I don't know how that happened. A director from New York was flown in to direct it. It was a musical about the history of Miami for the Queen of England's visit. A helicopter flew her in and there was security everywhere.

The ten of us in the cast stood in line to curtsey to the Queen. I did my very best ballet curtsey. She had an emerald the size of a chestnut on her index finger and a whole lot of other rings, rubies and sapphires. And her hands were see-through pale.

My singing solos had been changed to the cast singing with me. It was the worst musical, and she was sitting there in the first row surrounded by guards and the helicopter circling above. The whole time I'm thinking how terrible this must be for her to have to watch us. I had a new respect for her after that, because of all the horrid appearances she had to go to and sit there all patient with her hands in her lap, not yawning or itching her nose. I never did another musical after that.

During the summer I auditioned for commercials and acting

work. I got a part as a Swiss Miss hot chocolate girl. Two blonde braids, a short red-and-green quilted skirt, white tights and ear-muffs, standing in a park on a set made to look like the Swiss Alps with a snow machine and extras with wool sweaters and skis. It was July in Florida and 102 degrees. I just wanted to get home, take my tights and earmuffs off, and take a cold bath.

I booked a national commercial and got my Screen Actors Guild card. I was a stand-in for a lead in a movie for two months and told myself I would never be a stand-in again. Was an extra in a Levitz Furniture commercial that featured couches that re-minded me of the one in Chicago where the girls and I sat waiting to fit some man's description. And a bunch of other extra parts that I can't remember and that I hated doing. I was restless to move to LA, to be with Rilke and audition for parts that had meaning, not just sitting in fake snow in the Alps.

By the time I was ready to leave Miami, Cole had bought a house, started introducing me as his wife, and he'd even brought up the idea of a baby. My decision at six to never have a baby hadn't changed. People had always told me, "That will change one day." But it didn't. I don't think he ever believed me when I said I never wanted to get married and have kids. No man did.

I'll never forget that day at Miami International Airport. All six-four of him with his green eyes and broad shoulders. He was crying. I had never seen him cry before. I left most of my things with him and told him I would come back but knew I wouldn't and he must have known too. It was one of the hardest things I ever did, to leave while I was still in love but I knew if I didn't leave I would regret it. Rilke and I had been dreaming about being in LA together for too long. Ever since that first time we glued our hands together.

"Promise?" we'd ask one another.

"Promise."

Dove Bars and Madame Ava

Los Angeles – 22 years old – 1992

Rilke went to LA the day after she graduated high school just like she always said she would. She had already been there a year when I arrived. She was dancing burlesque at The Body Shop on Sunset Boulevard. I took a cab straight from LAX with my two suitcases to see her. Driving down Sunset past forest-green Range Rovers, matte-black Mercedes, Chateau Marmont, The Viper Room. Billboards for Freeze The Fat and Guess Jeans featuring a bronzed woman, hair blowing in all directions, looking over her shoulder at a tiger in the background.

I was let off in front of The Body Shop. 'Burlesque Review' on the marquee and flashing pink neon outlines of nude girls with tiny waists in high heels. I walked in and there was Rilke onstage for everyone to see with her glossy red lips and glitter on her boobs. She was always a good dancer and this wasn't all nude or topless, she had an act, and she even got a part in *Forrest Gump* as a featured dancer. A casting director had come in and seen her act and told her about the audition. She had five call-backs before she got the part. A famous actor used to come in and watch her too, and then they started dating. She had only slept with two men up until then, and when she didn't like him enough to make him her third they stopped seeing each other.

I stayed with her in a room she rented in Beachwood Canyon. I needed a car and to come up with money so we could find a place together.

"What about burlesque dancing?" Rilke asked.

I thought of myself up there on the stage dancing and all those people watching and I just couldn't imagine doing it. I just wanted to be with Rilke but I wasn't a good dancer. Even though I had grown up taking ballet lessons, and in the summers jazz and tap, I didn't have much talent and I had no rhythm. But Rilke, she mainly did jazz and in her class she always stood in front and got the solo. In ballet for me, I was usually the dancing tree in pink tights in the background. I was also too shy. The idea of one person seeing me dance almost naked was scary enough, let alone a whole audience.

"Do they have private dances?" I asked.

"It's burlesque, they don't have privates," she said.

I didn't even look at jobs for waitressing or hostessing. I went straight to the adult classified section of the *LA Weekly*. 'Make $1000 a night.' I'd make more than in Chicago.

"Two months then I'll quit, and never again," I told myself.

A week later I was sitting across from Madame Ava at The Silver Spoon on Santa Monica Boulevard.

"Beautiful you are," she said, looking at my dress.

I was wearing a purple mini dress cut low in the front. I'd worn it all the time when I'd been a call girl in Chicago. All the girls had worn short, tight dresses. It's what Mr. Ted wanted us to wear.

"My girls, dress only in good black suit," Madame continued. "Nothing to show too much."

I had never owned a suit before. How much did a good one cost? She must have guessed what I was thinking.

"Quality takes money," she said. "I give you money for suit and you go to Beverly Center. We take it out of your first night and you will be Lana. And get your nails done and hair must be straight. Yes, Lana you be." She opened the gold clasp of her Prada wallet and counted six crisp one-hundred-dollar bills.

How did she know I would not take that money and never see her again?

"My girls, the girls who are smart put away their money," she said, taking my hand in hers and inspecting my nails. "Some buy house."

I already knew I wasn't going to be doing this long. Just enough to get money for a car and a couple months' rent. I knew I wasn't the kind of girl who could make this a real business, invest my money and buy a house.

"You see, this, it is business. Now you go, go get the good suit. I call you Friday and you see, you start work."

She left in her mint-green Jaguar. I wondered how Madame got to be a Madame. I couldn't imagine that she was a call girl first. If she was, what was her first experience like? I was relieved to have a job and I was scared. Scared of how long I would do this, and the men. Would they be like in Chicago where I didn't have any men who frightened me? I thought of ballet man and if he had found a girlfriend yet. And Cole in Miami. I could go back to him and we could move to LA together one day.

That afternoon I went to the Beverly Center. Part of the building was covered with a Calvin Klein ad of a girl on all fours, wearing men's underwear and a white tank. I took the escalator six flights up and walked into Macy's.

"Would you like to try our new Elizabeth Taylor Escapade scent?" a girl with a high voice and long neck asked me.

"Where is your suit section?" I asked as I held out my wrist and she sprayed it lightly.

"What company?"

"Calvin Klein," I said but more as a question.

I picked out a few black skirt-suits. Five hundred for a suit? Would I make that back in a night?

"Would you like to try those on?" a woman with big hoop earrings and hair pulled back into a high ponytail asked.

I nodded.

She was about my age. What other kinds of jobs had she had?

"Starting a new job?" she asked, showing me to the dressing room.

I looked at her and didn't answer. "I think I need a blouse to try under."

The lighting in the dressing room was not as fluorescent as the Juniors department or Ross Dress For Less. I undressed, looking at myself in the three-way mirror. I would really need to watch what I eat now. Making money off my naked body. I sucked in my stomach and pulled the skin above my chest up, raising my boobs. I didn't have my mom's double Ds but they were natural, and I was never inclined to get fake ones even though I knew they could look and feel super natural because I had touched plastic ones with the girls in Chicago.

"Here's a couple blouses for you," the girl said. "I'll hang them on your door."

I lied to Rilke.

"It's an escort service where the girls don't sleep with the men, you're just supposed to lead them on and talk and let them massage you, but that's it."

I think she believed me. That Saturday night, Madame sent me to The Peninsula hotel. I dressed in a black pencil skirt, stockings, and a black, fitted blazer. The cab dropped me off in front of the hotel and I walked through the lobby, past the bar, couples drinking glasses of wine and martinis. In an hour I could stop at the 7-Eleven near my place for a dark chocolate Dove Bar and a packaged ham sandwich on honey wheat with American cheese, and then go home.

I walked past another woman wearing a suit. She was pretty, was she a call girl too? But she had a briefcase, she must have had a real job, but maybe she was a dominatrix and that briefcase had whips and restraints in it. Every time I saw a woman in a suit I wondered, lawyer or sex worker? The girls with platinum hair wearing cleavage dresses sitting at the bar with an older man, maybe they were just out on a normal date.

I took the elevator to the eighth floor, walked down the gold- and burgundy-wallpapered hallway. 803, 804, 805. I looked at the zigzag on the carpet. 806, 807. There was a silver tray outside 808. I looked down at my reflection in the tray. I was distorted. My blonde hair looked dry and frizzy. I stared down at my black heels. Maybe I'd get a milk chocolate Dove Bar instead of dark.

I hoped this man was not too unattractive.

Two knocks. He answered. He had light brown curly hair and was wearing a white robe with the initials BR embroidered in navy blue above his heart. His eyes were pale blue and real beady like some kind of bird and his lashes, they were so light it looked like he had none. He opened the door just enough to let me in. He didn't smile.

It was a big room opening onto a private patio with a Jacuzzi. On top of the TV in front of the bed was an envelope. He looked at me, moved the envelope in my direction. I put the envelope in the black sequined purse my mother sent to me. It was my grandma's, or maybe it was the one she got me from the Hadassah. I wondered how much was in the sealed envelope.

The man walked toward the Jacuzzi, untied his robe. There was something womanly about the way it fell to the floor and the way he stood there naked, one toe testing the water, then the other. He slid himself in, closed his eyes with his head tilted up as if the patio lights were real sunlight.

Those lashless eyes of his were still closed. "When you're ready."

I undressed. Looked at my pale naked self in the mirror. I was glad his eyes were closed. Right then he opened them and looked at me. A shiver went down my spine. I wanted to put my clothes on, go home. I didn't like this man. He waved me over. I walked towards him. He stared. My hands, my arms didn't know what to do. I didn't know where to look.

Then I was in the Jacuzzi next to him. He stroked himself. He stopped, took my hand and placed it on his dick. I don't know how but after that I was on the floor, lying there face-down with my nails digging into the carpet. He was on my back and his dick, he pierced himself into my ass and it was something terrible.

The quicker it was over the better, even if that meant pain. If I stopped him it would just prolong it. He was thrusting in and out fast, and I could feel he would cum soon.

I felt like I was six again with the old man and his floppy fish of a dick. I couldn't get out of the car then but I could leave now.

I could walk out the door. But thing of it was, I didn't stop him, and I was ashamed of myself for it. And after, I didn't even ask him for more money, I just left. No girl does that. No girl doesn't ask for more money.

Years later I saw him again. Not in real life but on TV. He was taking an award at the Oscars. It wasn't until he held the gold statue in his hand, the camera zooming in on his face that I remembered those beady lashless eyes of his. His thin lips moved as he thanked the Academy, but I didn't hear any words, I only felt a pit in my stomach so deep. I just stared at this man knowing I would never forget him.

I walked down the hallway. I stood in front of the gold-plated elevator, pressed the white "down" button. It lit up red. My fingers were pruned. The elevator opened, I stepped inside. I saw a reflection of myself in the speckled mirrored doors as they closed. Before I pressed the button the elevator opened and a dark-haired mother in a coral dress and matching button-up sweater and her little girl in monkey pajamas walked in. The little girl, her hand was in her mother's. I wanted to follow them back to their room and sleep on the floor near them. I wondered what this little girl would be when she grew up. She looked at me. My hair dripping onto my white button up, I stared down at her monkey slippers, furry cozy ones that matched her pajamas. Her mother looked at me. My eyes watered. The mom tugged at her daughter's hand as the elevator door opened.

The little girl looked back at me as they walked away. I tried to smile.

I got a taxi, he drove down Santa Monica Boulevard. Before dropping me off at home I had him stop at the 7-Eleven across the street from House of Pies, next to India's Kitchen. The cab driver parked in front of a payphone booth with no phone in it. The fluorescents in the 7-Eleven were extra bright. The man behind the counter, wearing a white turban and faded jeans, took money from a kid with a skateboard under his arm. The boy's armpit covered the middle of the skateboard but on one end of the skateboard it read, Live or Die. The boy walked out with an extra-large pink Slurpee.

There were tuna sandwiches on whole wheat, turkey with orange cheese. I chose the tuna. Mint chip, s'mores, coffee ice-cream. I wanted chocolate.

"We are out of chocolate," the man said.

I felt like crying, I did cry. I saw a Dove Bar, the tears stopped. I thought of bringing one home to Rilke but she wouldn't be home yet. If I bought two, I'd eat two.

I wished Rilke would be home.

Threesomes and Cocaine

One night Madame Ava called and told me, "I have husband and wife. Husband, he wants to watch."

I arrived at their condo in Brentwood wearing my uniform, a simple black suit. A woman with dyed blonde hair and a white slip with a fluffy pink fringe on the bottom answered the door. She kissed me on both cheeks, took my hand, and led me up the stairs to the bedroom. The carpet was a deep red. Dyed blue orchids and lavender-scented candles on the mantle, a mirror covered the ceiling above the bed. Her husband was naked, he was balding and had patches of hair on his stomach and the back of his hands. They reminded me of a couple who goes to swingers' parties. I had the impression I wasn't the first girl they had ordered. I wondered what line of work they were in, how long had they been together, was a threesome his idea or hers?

He sat in bed. Propped up with black satin pillows, a mirrored tray sat next to him with white powder on it. They snorted a couple lines, the lady handed me a rolled bill.

"It's just a little coke, honey," she said.

I'd never done coke and didn't want to try it that night.

The lady took the bill and put it in my hand. "We only buy the best. As you are."

I felt embarrassed to say no. I stuck the tip of the bill up my nose and snorted. I looked at the man.

"I'm just going to watch," he said, smiling.

"Take your shirt off," she said. "I'm getting a boob job this summer." She cupped my tits. "I want your size, not too big but not too small."

The man slid himself up close to the headboard, leaning back on the satin pillow. The bed was big enough, so she and I had lots of space. My head pointed one way, hers the other. This was my first time with a woman. I had never had a desire to be with one, but this seemed better than being with her husband.

"Keep your legs open so I can see," the man said, stroking his dick with his hairy hand.

She went down on me, I went down on her. I thought about how it felt having a guy lick me between my legs and the tingling sensation. I heard her tongue flicking away but I felt nothing. Pretending to like it I moaned, just enough but not too much, otherwise I thought I would sound fake since she hadn't been at it long. She made a purring sound. I wondered if she was faking it, too. She smelled like apple shampoo. What did I smell like to her?

After a couple minutes I was bored.

"You gotta get her going," the man said. "You got to lick her to life."

The coke settled in, my heart beat fast, and I wasn't bored but scared now, and I felt insecure that I wasn't doing a good job. I wanted it to be over like I always did when I was on a call.

"Come on," the man grunted. "Come on, get it going."

She purred louder, I moaned louder. She was just taking his orders, performing for him just like I was. It had to have been his idea to order a call girl.

"Now both you turn around," he said.

He had a camera in his hands, I turned my head away. At 2 a.m. I went back home. I wished I hadn't done the coke. Never again. Never again.

Rilke had left a piece of pie on the table. For a moment I felt normal, not scared.

Sorority Girl

I called Madame.

"Lana, darling," she said. "Tonight, you be UCLA sorority girl. Client, that's what he want."

An hour later I was on the 10 freeway headed to Westwood with my hair in a high ponytail, a yellow sweatshirt, jeans and running shoes. Underneath I had on white lacy underwear with pink bows on the side and a matching push-up bra, but not too push-up 'cause I didn't want to disappoint.

I took the Overland exit and headed north to Bentley Avenue. A 1970s building, champagne color, the color that reminded me of old ladies in Florida. I entered, it smelled like pork and mothballs, the lights in the hallway were too bright. #121. I knocked. A woman in the apartment opposite opened her door, she wore a blue velour bathrobe. She looked at me, I looked at her and her matching blue slippers. She closed the door. Her doormat said, Meow Welcome. I wanted to sit on her couch, curl up on it under a wool blanket, and drink Sleepytime Tea.

I knocked again. A small, young Asian guy cracked opened the door. His hair was black and neatly parted to the side.

"Lana?" he asked.

I nodded. He unlocked the chain and opened the door just enough to let me in. It was a studio apartment, books piled on a metal desk with a glass top, single mattress on the floor, a hot plate on top of a mini fridge in the corner. I wondered how he could afford a call girl.

He was wearing a UCLA sweatshirt, too-short khakis, and bare feet. The air in that room was not right. Thick. Felt like it needed moving around, like him and his books, they'd been in there too long. A window, I needed to open a window. I looked down at that mattress on the floor with its beige sheets that had a purple design on top. I didn't like the sheets, the beige depressed me. I thought of my pale blue ones at home, I wanted to be under them with my three pillows, like how my mom slept, a pillow on each side of her. Fortress.

"You don't fit my order," the guy told me.

And I was gone, just like that. I was relieved. I couldn't breathe in there. Some other girl, she'd be with him and his hot plate and beige sheets.

I went home. 11 p.m., three hours until Rilke came home. I wondered if the Asian found the sorority girl he wanted. I lay on the bed. An ambulance went by. Dogs howled; they sounded like coyotes and I just froze there on that bed in the dark, scared. I didn't think Madame would call me again and I didn't call her again that night to see if another man might want me. My mouth was dry, I curled up hugging my knees in close, cheeks wet.

The door unlocked, Rilke was home early. I jumped out of bed, and twenty minutes later Rilke and I were in the car eating the edges off apple fritters, throwing the middles out the window. When we got home we put on our roller skates, up and down the hallway we rolled. The lady below, *tap, tap* with a broomstick.

"Fuck you," we said.

Just like when we were kids, when we wrote fuck you notes and put them in every mailbox on Wisteria Street, even in the old Salmons who gave us candy corn.

There were other men. The Italian with his broad shoulders, straight white teeth and pinstriped starched shirt. He was in his thirties and looked too handsome to order a girl. His house was in Malibu by the ocean, steps above the rocks that led up to his door. Lots of white and bright lights. Red wine bottles, empty. The house and the bottles, nothing in them. He must have offered me a drink, maybe champagne. He sucked my toes one at a time, jerked off and came on my feet. We didn't have sex and the traffic, it wasn't bad going home. I was gone maybe two hours.

The hairless seventy-year-old man at the Beverly Hills Hotel. He was at least six-four, skinny spider legs and a hard protruding belly. He was wearing powder-blue pajamas and socks in a lobster print. He went into the bathroom and when he came out he was naked except for the lobster socks. I followed his example and went to the bathroom and undressed. When I came out he was sitting on the edge of the king-sized bed. He motioned for me to sit across from him in a dark oak chair.

"I just want to look at you," he said as he began to play with his balls. "You are so beautiful."

I watched him as he stroked his dick, trying to make it rise. His pale, hairless balls hung low. I felt like I was supposed to do something but when I began to touch myself or get up and walk toward him he motioned for me to stop. His hazel eyes never seemed to blink as he stared at me. My attention was fixed between his balls and the lobsters on his socks. He never got hard and he gave me two thousand for the hour.

I didn't tell Madame Ava about the extra money. I just gave her two hundred and hoped he'd call for me again, but he didn't.

Rilke Works for Madame Ava

Around the time when Rilke and I moved into our own place in Los Feliz she wanted to try out what I was doing since I was making money. It was the worst thing I ever did to her, to not tell her the truth about that. I don't know what I said, I was all worked up inside myself, but I tried to get her not to go.

"I will be Rosemary," she said.

Madame Ava told her, "Darling, the men, they do not want to be with a Rosemary. You will be a Beth."

So Rilke went out as Beth and when she came back she said, "He wanted to sleep with me, and I told him I'd dance for him. He wasn't happy about that, but I danced and took the money and left."

I'm sure at that point she knew I slept with them but she didn't say anything about it and she never went out again with any of Madame's men. Rilke was a lot more pure than me; she'd only slept with two guys. Not Madame Ava's, but her own guys who she liked for real.

Balls Like Japanese Eggplant

"He good client," Madame Ava said. "You do he want, he call again."

Ted. He'd ordered a young blonde. He lived downtown. It was noon on a weekday. I drove down Third Street, past Korean BBQ, Uncle Bob's, Thai Massage and Mani/Pedi twenty-dollar special, the courthouse and the county jail towards Olvera Street. I thought maybe I'd treat myself to carne asada on Olvera afterwards. I wondered how long this would take. I parked in a five-dollar lot at Spring and 8th, walked across the street. The doorman had me write my name in the visitor list. Lana. What was my last name? Madame Ava hadn't given me one. Jones, I'd be Jones.

I took the elevator to the 11th floor. The brass elevator door engraved with an elephant opened, I walked down the gray concrete hall. #1108. I smelled incense. Nag Champa. Looked at my feet. Black Marshalls stockings, there was a run in the big toe. I slid my foot out of the heel, squatted down to arrange the stocking so the hole was under my toe, slid the shoe back on. The door opened. A tall, thin man with a gray goatee stood over me.

I stood up. His eyes were blue and he looked at me with a slight smile. He was wearing dark blue jeans rolled at the cuff, bare feet, and a gray V-neck sweater. It looked like cashmere. He didn't look like a Ted. Bookcases divided the loft into a bedroom and a large living room with concrete floors covered in Afghan rugs. Floor-to-ceiling windows from one end to the other.

"Vodka is okay?" he asked.

"With orange juice," I said, looking at his books.

Foucault, Bukowski, Flaubert. I didn't picture men who dialed up call girls to light Nag Champa or read Flaubert.

An hour later he was lying naked on the coffee table, a thick slab of wood with iron legs. His feet and hands were tied. He was blindfolded and I was whipping him with a riding crop.

I thought of being a call girl in Chicago and what one of the men had said, "Talk dirty to me."

How when I couldn't do it he was nice about it and we went for donuts instead at his favorite bakery at 3 a.m. as they were baking them.

"The owner's an old friend," he said.

In the alleyway, we walked in through the back entrance. Donuts drowning out the smell from the dumpsters. I was wearing a gold lamé dress and heels. I wondered if he brought other girls here when they couldn't get the dirty words out and if he'd pay me for the night even though he didn't get off. We sat in his car eating cinnamon twists and raspberry-filled donuts with white powder on top.

Ted was on the wood table.

"Harder, Lana," he said.

As I brought the whip down the sound of his voice jolted me as if I had drifted off somewhere else and wasn't conscious of what I was doing. I was surprised that I didn't feel uncomfortable whipping this thin man. He was helpless lying there and he couldn't do anything to me, I was the one who had control.

I thought about how carne asada and vodka didn't go together and decided I wouldn't go to Olvera Street after.

"Tie up my balls," he said.

He had me whip them. I imagined his balls turning purple the next day like a Japanese eggplant. I wondered if he thought I was doing a good job, if he'd call Madame Ava for Ms. Lana again. Probably not, part of me didn't care, Madame Ava could send for some other blonde. I poured wax on his nipples and stroked his dick. He looked pleased, maybe he would tell Madame I was good. That I was a good call girl. But why was I even questioning that? It wasn't my ambition to grow up and be good at whipping balls. I was twenty-two years old. This is not what I had envisioned for myself as a little girl. I thought about my grandma, aunt, and great grandma, how they had been lawyers and opened the first female family law office in New York. Why, while Ted lay there, was I thinking about them now, when I hadn't after all these years?

On the way home I stopped for gas at the 76 Station on Sixth Street across from Bargain Bin and Shoes For Less. A woman with matted brown hair, a yellow raincoat and one red flip-flop was sitting on the curb. She had a wheelchair with her clothes folded in the seat of it with a black garbage bag on top. She wore a green knapsack with lavender stuffed into a half empty jar of Skippy's peanut butter. I always wanted to eat Skippy as a kid, not the unsalted kind with nuts in it that my dad got from the health food store. The woman was maybe fifty. I wondered what she was doing at my age and where I would be when I'm fifty.

After filling the tank I got back in the car and opened the envelope. Ted's money. My money, I started counting the twenties. Looked at lavender lady sitting there. She looked at me, I opened the car door to give her money. She walked over, I handed it to her. I put the key in the ignition, drove to Alvarado, headed to Carl's Jr. for dessert.

"A chocolate malt please," I said at the drive through window. "With whipped cream."

The malt tasted good. I licked the whip cream off the top as I drove past MacArthur Park. The white cream was comforting. Rilke and me, we had lots of malts in the summer. Walking hand in hand under the palm trees to Woolworth's at Gulf Gate Mall where we'd sit at the counter on red swivel stools and stick long red- and white-striped straws into a snow of cream stained red on top from where we picked off the maraschino cherry. Tall glasses with Coca Cola printed on the side. The Woolworth's waitress in her pink and white checkered apron smiling at us with red lipstick on her teeth.

The Wild Goose

It was a Friday night in November. Rilke was at The Body Shop. I sat on the edge of my bed in boxers alone. I hadn't picked up the phone to call Madame Ava for work in two weeks. And when she called I didn't pick up. I just stared at the phone letting it ring. My head crowded with men. The lashless Jacuzzi man, Ted and the whip, the cocaine couple, Malibu man with his empty house and liquor bottles, the hairless 70-year-old man and all the men in Chicago. It hadn't been long but I felt all used up.

Cars passed on Franklin, each one, vibrating through the bare room and hardwood floors. Bare except for the bed Rilke and I shared. Before we shared it, we had bunk beds that we bought at Kids Furniture World next to Thai Fantasy. We set up the bunk in the dining room, turning our bedroom into a workout room to lose weight but that didn't work out, the losing weight. We got rid of the bunks and the weights, bought a Queen mattress and moved back into the bedroom.

The cars passed. I imagined the people in them. I wanted to be with them, sit in their backseat, go wherever it was they were going. What was I supposed to do now? Stay home? It didn't feel like a home, not without Rilke. My sheets, I thought about getting under them, but the apartment...the cars, the wood floors...

Rilke got a part in a movie, *Showgirls*. She didn't almost get the part because the director wanted her to be naked but she said she wouldn't take her g-string off. All the other girls in the movie took off their clothes.

I visited her on set at Raleigh Studios. A black soundstage set up to look like a strip club, circular glossy tables with ash-trays half filled, beer and vodka bottles behind a black bar. Pink and red strobe lights, a tattooed bartender with a belly hanging over his silver eagle belt buckle. Girls. Blondes, brunettes, redheads wearing black fishnets, five-inch platform heels giving lap dances to thin men in nylon jogging pants. Rilke wore a pink-sequined bra and matching panties in her main scene where she had one line, "Nomi, do my boobs look bigger?" She had rehearsed that line a whole lot with me.

"Cut," the director said.

I'd visit her on set, at break time Rilke and I ate powdered donuts and lox at the craft service table. The director, Paul Verhoeven, would come talk to us sometimes. He told us he'd put us both in his next movie. That never happened.

Rilke had a couple more weeks of filming. She wasn't very happy because she ate too many donuts on set and felt fat. The other girls didn't eat donuts. I spent most days waiting for her and thinking about how I couldn't keep doing what I was doing. I never called the Madame again. (It wasn't hard.)

When Rilke finished filming we got a job at a strip club together off of Fletcher Drive on the East side, The Wild Goose. It felt like a step up from Madame Ava. The Wild Goose was good, it was off the tracks, I felt hidden and safe. Rilke and I had each other, we got to be together all the time. That's when we became Lola and Claudia.

At first I served apple juice. No liquor or beer, it was nude and only topless places served alcohol. Girls danced, men watched and I took orders for juice wearing a Swiss Alps apron, lacy underwear, two blonde braids, pink and too glossy Wet N' Wild lip gloss from the Dollar Store and bobby socks. The kind with the ruffle, like six-year-olds wear, but I wasn't six, I was almost twenty-three.

Four nights a week we went to work in our matching blue flannel bathrobes and fuzzy slippers that our mom sent. We'd pack up our MOMA bags with caramel rice-cakes and heels. At three am, we'd go home and wash off our make-up. Rilke would get back to reading *War and Peace* and me a Somerset Maugham novella, or I'd write in my journal. Ever since I was a little girl I had kept a journal, I had boxes of them. Writing was just something I did to help me through the day, words kept me company. Sometimes I'd write bits of conversation down, what I ate for breakfast or about the morning glories out my window. I'd think of my dad and him telling me about when he first started writing poetry.

"In high school I was part of a gang. I was in charge of sending out postcards in code to everyone. Later, in the navy I wrote love letters home for my shipmates. I sat at the bow of the ship, reading TS Eliot in the night. I loved words."

There was a part of me that envied writers. That they could do it anytime, anywhere, but the aloneness of sitting with words scared me. I still wanted to be an actress. I liked that acting involved being around people. A collaborative process. But there was a part of me that questioned if acting really was my passion.

Rilke didn't like to write and I didn't like long books like she did. Most things we liked the same, but not books or boys. She liked a book that went on and on, and short guys. I liked short books and tall guys. We were perfect together, Rilke and me.

Sisters of Playboy

During the day we tried to work on our acting: getting head shots taken in blue denim shirts, sending them out to agents, getting no response, sending out more, cold-calling agents.

"You need better head shots," they told us.

We'd save more money, get more head shots, then hear the same thing again from another agent.

"We already have too many blondes," they'd say.

There was one agent who didn't say that. This Russian guy on Hollywood Boulevard near Mann's Chinese where Mickey Mouse stood and waved to people from Idaho and Nebraska as they looked at the sidewalk of stars, stepping on the ones they didn't know, onto the next who they did. His office was across the street from the Hollywood Wax Museum in a 1970s building. Out front were vendors and their racks of postcards of James Dean, Brando, and Marilyn, and coffee cups that said, 'I Love LA'.

He wore a lopsided toupee. I just wanted to lean on in and straighten his hairpiece out the first time he called us in.

Faded head shots a little warped and yellow at the corners were tacked on the wall behind his desk where he sat looking through piles of newer headshots.

"You girls, I got something for you. Sisters of Playboy."

We didn't know what Sisters of Playboy meant but we liked the sisters part. We were to report to the *Playboy* offices on Beverly Boulevard the next morning. We really didn't like getting up early so that was already not a good thing. That meant we'd have to get up extra early if we were going to look right. Taking a bath, cause we always took a bath instead of a shower, shaving, washing our hair and setting it in rollers, nairing our upper lips.

The next day we drove off in our leather mini-skirts, Fredrick's shoes, black lace bras. Rilke in a pink cashmere midriff and for me, a see-through red polka-dot blouse with a puffy kind of collar.

We parked in the underground garage, taking the elevator to the first floor. A woman in a white fluffy sweater and red lips sat behind a marble desk with a phone in her hand.

"Please hold. *Playboy*, how may I direct your call?" she asked, while pointing to us to sign in. "Just a moment please," she said, pressing one of the red flashing lights on the phone.

"We're here for Sisters of Playboy," I told her.

"Fifth floor to your left. Conference room A5."

We checked our makeup in the mirrored elevator. Applied extra pink gloss. The elevator stopped, doors opened. Rows of cubicles, people on the phone, tables with glossy nudes laid out. Walking down the hall we didn't say anything to each other. I didn't feel so steady in my heels. Room A5. The door was closed. I knocked. A blonde woman in a black skirt suit and green-framed glasses opened the door. It was a big room with a glossy oval conference table filling most of it, black padded leather chairs set all around, the chairs empty except for a man sitting at the farthest end in a navy blue suit, yellow bow tie and matching silk handkerchief in his breast pocket. She took a seat next to him. Laid out in front of her were two eight-by-ten pictures of Rilke and me.

"Tell us about yourselves," she said, taking off her glasses.

I hoped Rilke would say something. She didn't and neither did I.

"Well, let's start by telling you a little about this segment," the man said. "As you know this is Sisters of Playboy. What we're aiming to do here is capture sisters in their natural habitat. Nothing forced. We want who you really are to come through."

"Essentially, giving the viewers a look at you doing hobbies in your bikinis or topless," the lady said. "Tell us about your hobbies?"

We were still standing there in front of that conference table and I wondered if we were supposed to sit down or keep standing. The lady and the man, they seemed kind of far away with the distance of the desk between us.

"We like to roller skate and read," Rilke said.

"Excellent." Bow tie man nodded his head, writing on a legal pad. "At the Santa Monica Pier?"

"No," I said. "We like to roller skate in our apartment."

"I see," the man said. "Well, the important thing is you can roller skate. What magazines do you read?"

"We don't like magazines," I said.

"Oh, so when you say reading, what is it you like to read? What are reading now?"

Rilke looked at me, then back at the man. *"Remembrance of Things Past."*

"I'm reading *The Bell Jar.*"

Bow tie man wrote something down again and the lady turned and whispered something to him.

"If you wouldn't mind now taking off your clothes," she said.

I wanted them to turn the fluorescents off. Rilke and I looked at each other as she took her cashmere off and I started unbuttoning my blouse. We unzipped our skirts and stood there in our heels, underwear and bra.

"Everything, please," the lady said.

I stared at the lady's hands. She had big wrists. I wondered if she had big ankles, I couldn't see her feet from where I was standing. I thought of one girl at the strip club. The beautiful Swede who had thick ankles that didn't fit the rest of her body.

"Turn around," bow tie man said.

We turned around with backs to them. I thought back to the first time I became a call girl in Chicago. How the man who got the men for us girls asked me to undress in his office after I met him for the interview at the Italian restaurant where he ate lots of garlic bread. Standing there with Rilke, I wanted to pick up my clothes and walk out the door.

"Okay, girls, you can put your clothes back on. We thank you for coming in today."

Two weeks later the Russian agent called.

"My girls," he said. "*Playboy*, they want you."

We had never asked how much it paid, assuming it would be pretty good money, but it didn't. Something like $400 for the day. We decided not to do it and to never call or see that agent with his toupee again. We also decided, any auditions we went on from now on had to be with clothes. Working at a strip club in the valley next to the railroad tracks and the LA River, that's where we felt more comfortable. Where no one would know or see us. Our acting was separate, something we wanted to take seriously.

Strip

I stopped serving soda and changed my name to Claudia. Rilke was Lola. I started giving lap dances in a private red booth. It was mirrored with blue lights. My first man smelled of garlic and wore thin nylon jogging pants. I felt his hardness, forty dollars I told myself. I tried not to look at him. In the mirror I saw a tall girl with black hair to her waist giving a shower dance. A man was hosing her down, aiming high between the legs. I saw Rilke too, hanging nude on a pole. I closed my eyes and imagined her and me when we were little practicing tap dance routines and playing Yahtzee.

After a summer Rilke and I moved on to The Gentleman's Club. Prettier girls, more money, more competition: Celeste with her little tanned bum, big auburn hair, fake boobs and black patent leather thigh boots. Jasmine. Blonde hair, boobs, long legs. Lily, the tiny Asian who looked fourteen, wore bobby socks and pleated school uniform mini-skirts. Dusty with her nude splits, back flips and tricks on the pole. Taylor and her fishnet skin suit. Candy just walked out onstage nude with her bare feet and boobs.

Daytime girls, a little heavier, a little older, spread their legs while men ate the stale lunchtime pizza strip special. These girls had kids, made less money, danced at 2 p.m. on Wednesdays for regulars. Big Red came in at 4 p.m., sat on a stool in his blue and white overalls with a supply of Big Red chewing gum set out next to his juice. He stayed until closing. Having a slow day? You could count on Big Red for a twenty-dollar dance. You could always count on him for a dance and cinnamon gum.

I avoided cute, younger guys who came in on a Saturday night for bachelor parties. Wasn't sure I was pretty enough to ask if they wanted a dance. Asian men who came on buses, they all liked me, and I was sure to make money when I saw the buses. City workers and white men didn't like me. They liked Beth, Taylor, and Dusty, who acted like this was a really fun thing to do.

We seemed to do well in the beginning. They liked to see us together.

"If Claudia and Lola don't do well," the girls used to say, "You know it's a bad night."

The girls never traded clothes with us.

"Maybe that's because we don't buy clothes at Fredrick's of Hollywood like the other girls," I told Rilke.

We wore bras and undies from Marshalls.

"Or maybe it's because we're curvier and need to lose weight," Rilke said.

We ate rice cakes, frozen yogurt, and sticky rice. On Saturday nights we allowed ourselves to go to IHOP on Santa Monica Boulevard for blueberry pancakes. We were curvier than the other girls. We never saw them eat.

"Maybe we should stop going to IHOP," I told Rilke, "And try a seven-day fast."

"Let's first try with a diet," Rilke said.

The first time we'd ever tried to diet was when Rilke was six and I was nine and we wanted to look good for a big dance recital at The Pink Elephant.

"A Yoplait strawberry yogurt for lunch and an Italian salad at Crusty Louie's for dinner," we agreed.

Sometimes we'd break down and go to Waffle House, then we'd ride our bikes up and down the street and leave the 'fuck you' notes in our neighbors' mailboxes. After, we'd come home and pull chairs in front of the mirror in our mom's room and examine our butts. We were worried of having flat, square butts like our mom.

"I'll kill myself if I have a bum like hers," we'd say.

Our friend Ashley Grant was eight and took gymnastics. We'd invite her over just to watch her walk around in a bathing suit with her perfect tanned butt. Little girls acting like two creepy old men. When she'd leave we would be sulky that our mom gave us these imperfect butts.

We slept with ribbons tied around our head and under our chins to prevent double chins. In the morning, we picked grapefruits off the tree in the backyard to burn extra fat. Later we'd forget about all that and go for sundaes at Woolworth's, roller skate in the lanai, and listen to the crickets.

Sometimes, when our mom was out with one of her men, we would sit on her Queen-sized bed with the plaid blanket. We sliced Granny Smith apples and break off a piece of a dark chocolate bar and watch Jane Fonda exercise videos. Jane wore tight turquoise spandex all over and a magenta headband and she'd lift one leg then the other and with each leg lift we'd eat another slice.

Jane would tell us, "If you really want to burn those extra

calories, strap your weights on."

"Doesn't she remind you of Mom?" we'd always ask each other.

When the apples and chocolate were gone we'd get under the covers and wait for our mom.

At the strip club we tried a lot of diets.

The Rice Krispie diet. We'd buy marshmallows, butter and Rice Krispie cereal, melting the butter on the stove and stirring it all together. We'd ask people if they'd make them for us, drive to the valley and Ed Debevick's on La Cienega Boulevard for them. Each one had a different consistency. It had to do with the ratio of marshmallows to butter and temperature. Too many marshmallows, not enough butter, not enough marshmallows, stale Rice Krispies.

One time we made them on acid. That was the best batch ever, but we didn't really like acid so we didn't do that again.

The AM/PM soft serve ice-cream diet. Allowing ourselves two trips a day to the AM/PM gas station across the street from the Church of Scientology. We tried other AM/PM locations but the consistency was wrong. We'd pull down on the lever of that machine, filling the cup as high as we could with chocolate and vanilla mixed together, then an extra dab of just chocolate on top.

The potato diet. Peeling a dozen potatoes at a time. Boil, cut, fry. We ate six a day with ketchup and I Can't Believe it's Not Butter spray.

The egg white diet. Egg whites, as many as we wanted all week, and one chocolate cake each on the weekend.

We gained weight on most of the diets. The girls in the strip club even said we gained weight, that's when we tried Weight Watchers.

"You have to be a certain weight to join," the lady said as she weighed us in. "You don't qualify."

We went to another location where we arrived with weights strapped to our ankles and bandaged to our stomachs and wore baggy sweatshirts. That worked.

The following week, on weigh-in day, we didn't wear the weights.

"This is astonishing," the lady said, as she adjusted the scale. "You both lost ten pounds."

Weight Watchers was very hard. We couldn't keep to the point system and were hungry all the time. We weren't allowed frozen yogurt, too many points. That was a problem because we lived for frozen yogurt. Calling in to Penguins and The Big Chill every morning to hear the recorded message.

"Today, Tuesday, December 8th, the flavors of the day are peppermint palm, vanilla bean..."

We drove an hour every day from Los Feliz to Westwood, and if the flavors in the valley were good, then to Studio City. Cookies N' Cream and Heath Bar Crunch meant two trips. We sat in the parking lot in our 4Runner that we shared. We'd traded in our two matching Tercels for the one car since we went everywhere together. Sometimes we'd be so full from the frozen yogurt we'd just take a nap in front of Penguins. Wake up, go home, set our hair in rollers, put on our blue bathrobes and head to the strip club. On the way, we'd put in our teeth-bleaching trays, spitting out the excess bleach in the empty frozen yogurt cup.

The yogurt diet wasn't working. We talked to Athena at the strip club. She had a butt like Ashley Grant.

"What's your workout routine?" we asked her.

"Workout? Meth and lipo," she said.

Three months later Rilke and I were recovering from lipo-suction on our bums. All the other girls at the strip club had done something, not just Athena. We just couldn't live with the way our bums looked any longer.

We'd found Dr. Renisch in the *LA Weekly*, voted one of the top ten liposuction doctors in LA. We had to wait two months for an appointment. For the consultation we stood naked while Dr. Renisch asked us, "What exactly are you not happy with?"

"The under part," I said. "You see how there's no line sepa-rating the bum from the hamstring?"

"I see," he said, taking a purple marker out of his breast pock-et. "I could do a little here and here." He drew circles under our bums. "More and more young girls like you are coming in."

"We can't live like this anymore," Rilke said. "We've tried diet and exercise."

"And my upper arms," I said. "I'm very unhappy with them."

He drew purple circles on my arms. The nurse came in and took pictures. "You will need someone to help you home and take care of you the first few days," the nurse said. "And you'll need to wear a girdle for three weeks while you heal."

When we had moved to LA our mom started visiting once a year. She would stay with us four or five days. We'd always use that time to make our place look better. She was really good at it.

"Less is better," she'd say.

Sometimes we weren't very nice, like with the liposuction.

"Mom, this time while you're visiting we're getting lipo-suction, and we need to have someone to help after."

She had made her ticket for ten days despite us telling her to keep it to five. We knew ten days was too long to have her stay with us. By the fifth day, after we were healing and coming down from the pain medication, we told her she couldn't stay with us any longer. I think we justified telling her to leave because we felt resentful that she had always put her men before us. It was, and still is, hard to admit this. I always felt guilty for any mixed feelings I had about her, and there were times she had been there. Like when I had called her crying from the payphone in Montreal.

I still feel bad about sending our mom to a hotel after lipo. When I apologized to her years later, she said, "Oh it was fine. I remember I met a nice man who took me out for Matzo Ball soup."

Three weeks later, with the girdles off, we stood on the rim of the bathtub, inspecting our butts in the mirror above the sink.

"We have a line under our butt," Rilke said. "It's beautiful."

The thing is, after lipo, while we were healing we gained weight. The result gave us a muffin-top effect. Extra weight around the hip area above the butt.

"We should have had Dr. Renisch point that needle up while we were at it," I said. "What's wrong with us? I can't believe we didn't do that."

We were very upset with ourselves.

"Seven pounds by the end of the month," we agreed. "Nothing but an apple for breakfast, one cup of sticky rice for lunch, and a chicken breast for dinner. And if we're really starving and feel like we're going to run to Lucky's for cake, rice cakes. But only in an emergency."

By day ten we were ordering sundaes at the McDonald's drive thru.

"Hold the ice cream, nuts, cherries and whip cream," I told the woman in the window.

"Just the caramel?" the lady would ask.

"That's right, just caramel."

We sat in the McDonald's lot at Vermont and Santa Monica in between Home Depot and a porn theater. *Debbie Does Dallas* was playing. Eating our warm cup of caramel, Rilke said, "We need a jump start to lose a few pounds right away."

"Let's ask Athena about her meth diet," I said.

"That's a good idea, she's gotta have speed. You can hardly get her out of that bathroom, and after work she's always at the laundromat."

"We're probably, like, the only girls who haven't tried it. We'll do it for one week and one week only, just to get rid of the muffin top."

We didn't diet anymore once we got on speed. Eating wasn't interesting, not even frozen yogurt.

We did meth for a month, didn't eat. Crushing the crystals and cutting the lines, the burn in the nose as I snorted it, I loved the ritual the first time. We started to be in bad moods, got clumsy onstage and in the private booth dancing, losing balance, and we didn't lose a pound. Everybody loses weight on meth, not us. We got on Fen-Phen, a diet drug. We got skinnier like Dusty, Jasmine and Athena.

We thought we looked better.

"I think we should cut our hair," I said.

"Maybe it will help us get better auditions and taken seriously. Let's dye it black too," Rilke said.

We began to make less money and bought hundred-dollar

wigs on Hollywood Boulevard. Me, a platinum waist length wig with bangs that shifted to one side when I danced. Rilke, a chestnut fall attached to the back of her head, she'd swing it around like a sexy pony onstage. Rilke started to make money again with her ponytail wig and good dancing. Not me. I got real sensitive and sad, getting skinnier and skinnier with that Fen-Phen, sitting on the side and crying with my big blonde Hollywood Boulevard wig.

I had Frank, though. He followed me from The Wild Goose to The Gentleman's Club. He never asked the other girls for a dance. He only came to see me, first as Irina or Ava or whatever my name was at The Goose, now as Claudia. I wanted to be Alexis but that name was already taken. Frank brought me flowers, Shalimar, and money for private dances. He was an Asian architect with a big belly, he wanted to bring me to The Magic Castle for dinner and shopping at Victoria's Secret, but I kept it to the club and private dances. Sometimes I let him touch me when the bouncer wasn't looking.

There was another man who came to see me regular, I thought he was a director at the studio nearby. He was quiet and didn't sit at the stage. Tall and thin with gray hair in a short ponytail, narrow nose and small eyes that looked like they saw a lot. I liked him right away. He came in, sat at the bar, and ordered an apple juice. I never went up to him, letting him take his time until he looked at me and started to walk to the back. I'd follow him behind the black velvet curtain, taking his long thin hand and leading him to a mirrored private dance booth with the fake red leather chair.

Rocco the bouncer, an ex-football-player, had his hand on the black velvet curtain, keeping his eye on me as I straddled the director in my Swedish barmaid outfit until the song was over. I had sex with Rocco once. I didn't know he had a fiancée. She climbed through the window of his apartment and chased me out.

I ran through the yard with his litter of pit bulls running after me and barking.

One time after work Rilke and I went to a Japanese restaurant between the studio and the club. We pulled on our green hospital pants that we always wore, tee shirts, and knotted our hair on top of our heads so it sprayed out like fountains. There was the director eating sushi with a woman and a little girl. I walked right up to him with my rice in a white paper bag that was stamped with a red smiley face and said, "Hi."

He just stared at me. I never saw him again.

Rilke Meets Squid

Rilke and I didn't spend as much time together after she met Judah, AKA Squid.

We met Squid at a daytime drug party in Sun Valley at a 1970s house with fake grass, sliding glass doors, and a cement backyard. The party looked boring, ten people lying on the couch, standing around, leaning against the fridge. A girl with blonde hair, red pleated miniskirt, and bare feet blended us a mushroom shake. We'd done everything, but not mushrooms. Rilke drank hers out of a coffee cup, I drank mine out of a white mug that said 'Number One Granny' on it. We waited for the hit from the mushrooms, went to the bathroom. As we took turns peeing, we both fell on the furry bright green bath mat laughing, then back to the kitchen. That's when Squid walked in and looked at us. His hair buzzed close to his scalp. What hair there was, was dyed leopard.

"Want to see something?" he asked.

He yanked down his zipper, pulled out his uncircumcised dick, took a pencil from his back pocket, and stuck it through his pierced foreskin. Rilke and Squid liked each other right off.

Squid visited her at the Gentleman's Club. He'd spend the night at our place, I'd hear them having sex in the living room and again more sex. He'd lock himself in the bathroom coughing and running the water. Squid was a heroin addict. He called Rilke from jail one day to get him, and I went with her. His mother showed up, took us all to Denny's. In the middle Squid got sick and left. We sat there with Squid's mother eating grilled cheese on white bread not knowing what to say.

Squid lived in Sylmar, far as you can go in the valley, with his grandma who wrote bad checks. He had the bedroom. She wore mumu dresses with bunny prints, made boxed pineapple upside-down cake, and slept on the couch. On the other couch was another grandma. They called each other grandma. At night they pushed the couches side by side. During the daytime, they sat in that house in Sylmar.

While Rilke and Squid had sex and fought, drove back from Los Feliz to Sylmar, then Sylmar to Los Feliz and back for more sex, I continued to lose weight and lose my shape. I took more and more Fen-Phen from doctors in Koreatown, the Valley, and Western Boulevard. I wore electric-blue jogging pants with gray flannels underneath. I fried up three or four bags a day of frozen vegetables with curry from the Armenian market in the kitchen that was painted black. The only sound: cars on Franklin Boulevard. I was depressed.

Rilke moved out with Squid, I looked for another place. She said go anywhere but Miracle Mile. I found a one-bedroom in Miracle Mile. The landlady Bertha was Jewish and old.

"Honey, you strip for a living?" she asked. "You move in. I know you make money. But no visitors."

She meant it. No visitors. She monitored the front entrance

in her blue fuzzy slippers, her thin red hair standing on end.

I had the back corner apartment with industrial carpeting. Looking out the two large living room windows I could open the screen and touch the stucco. Same view from the kitchen, it wasn't painted black.

My bedroom overlooked the old neighbor in his yarmulke. He stood on his porch with his thin pale legs in dingy boxers hanging wet undershirts on a wheel-in clothing line. On his windowsill an old tape played sad Jewish music. He must've had a wife. I wondered when she died and how long this mourning music would go on. How much longer could I strip and eat curried vegetables?

I liked this guy Bobby, an actor from New Mexico. I hadn't liked a guy since I left Cole and it had been a year since I'd had sex. I saw him walking down the street I lived on. His dark hair hanging over his face, never looking up, only down at the pavement. He worked at Buzz Coffee on Beverly Blvd. He didn't like me as much as I liked him but I hoped one day he would.

"My ex girl, she just up and left," he told me. "My heart still hurts."

I wanted his heart to hurt for me. Sometimes he spent the night, he kept his jeans on, I kept my underwear on and we'd just kiss. I didn't want to sleep with him too fast. Once we played pool at Hollywood Billiards, I wore a blue cashmere dress and he said I looked pretty. Another time we went to the movies in the middle of the day and it was raining. When I got cold he took off his jacket and let me wear it.

"I think this could work," he said as we sat side-by-side in the movie theater.

The next day he called to tell me he got back together with his ex. I cried and later I walked down the street with a cat that someone had left by my door a few months earlier. The cat had looked depressed so I let it stay with me. I knocked on Bobby's door and asked if the cat could stay at his place for the night. I wasn't really going anywhere I just wanted to see him. I went back to my apartment, sat in the butterfly chair trying to block out the sad Jewish music.

There was a knock at the door.

"Squid," Rilke cried, "I walked in on him shooting up. Last month he told me he quit."

She moved one street over from me to Cochran, next to Staples and Sally's Beauty. The same day she moved our cars got repossessed. We ended up sharing a 1988 Mazda, every time we turned a corner it screeched. Sometimes we parked it down the street so nobody saw us in it.

Rilke was trying to get over Squid and I was trying to quit stripping. I thought about acting and how I hadn't done one thing since I'd been in LA. It didn't even sound interesting anymore, I knew if I really loved it I'd find a way to do it, like be in a play, but I heard you could make money doing extra work in movies and it wasn't hard to do. I signed up with Central Casting and spent mornings calling in for work. Most of the time it was a recording.

"Call for homeless teens."

"Two African American males."

"Young, hip club goers and a Vietnam vet-type with no arm."

If I fit the description I drove to the valley in the Mazda. If I didn't fit I'd go to San Fernando Boulevard to strip.

The Little Boy in the Blue Jumper

Rilke did get over Squid. She fell in love with an Austrian-Jamaican man. They got married at a friend's house in the hills by a priest they had found in the back of the *LA Weekly*. "Priest on Wheels," the ad said. It was a small outdoor wedding and our mom was there, and Rilke's dad, Paul. Rilke looked so beautiful in her simple silk white dress with her long hair loose and the man she loved by her side. Unlike me she had always wanted to get married and have kids.

"We're moving to New York," she said the day of the wedding.

When she told me that, my whole body froze and I couldn't hold back the tears. It felt like when we were kids, all those summers of having to say goodbye to each other, only this time Rilke was leaving.

"What will happen when one of us falls in love?" we'd always asked one another.

"We'll just have to tell our husband he has to take the sister too."

We said that for a lot of years but we knew the truth, it would be hard.

When she left I stopped stripping. Nobody wants a crying stripper, and I couldn't do it without her. Something in me went wrong. It was like I was two again but I was in my late twenties and feeling maybe what I felt like when I was two and my mom left and I didn't have any words just the memory of arms reaching out of the crib for her. Reaching, crying, but she never came. I don't remember who did.

When I was ten I saw a movie. I don't remember anything about it except one scene and I'm not sure if it's exactly how it was in the movie but what stayed with me since then was the image of a mom and her two year old boy. A white house with a pebble path and long driveway. The boy is looking out the window, little hands and face pressed against the glass. He's wearing a blue jumper. The mom, she's walking down the path, not looking back. Skirt to the knees, bare calves, heels, *click*, *click* on the pebbles.

The boy is crying, "Mom."

She does not turn back, gets in her car. The boy is gone from the window, his handprints left on the glass from the fog of his breath. He runs out the front door, his face is red, the tears, the cries, his arms outstretched before him, reaching towards her. She is driving away, he's running after her. The blue strap of his jumper comes undone, snot runs down his nose, he can hardly breathe.

"Mom, Mom."

She does not come back.

I was ten and in that movie theater and I couldn't breathe, I couldn't stop crying. Shaking. The image of that boy at the window, hands pressed against the glass, him running after her, I carried that image of him with me for so many years, I could still hear the sound of her heels on the pavement, *click, click* as she walked away. I couldn't let it go. Is that how I felt when I was two and my mom went away?

All I ever wanted was for my mom to be there. Growing up, that one month out of the year going to see her, I wanted to feel special, to be seen. I saw moms packing lunchboxes for their kids in commercials, kids who got angry at their moms in movies. Getting angry, that seemed like a privilege to me. I was too scared, scared that she wouldn't be there if I ever got angry. But she was already not there. I have pictures of Rilke and I standing with our mom in matching gold lamé shorts under a palm tree and me with her on my sixteenth birthday. She had invited kids from the neighborhood, nobody I knew, to Sophie's, a French restaurant. I sat at the head of the table with my crew cut that Mom didn't like and Rilke, she had her two long braids that Mom did like, and she got to stay and I was always the one that had to go away. I felt guilty for these thoughts because maybe I was wrong, maybe she was there every July, I didn't know, but I did remember the goodbyes at Bradenton airport. I didn't like being left, or airports. I always got lost on the way, everybody knew not to call me to take or pick them up from LAX. Something always happened along the way.

And now Rilke was leaving. With her there, she was who I held onto. We were enmeshed, I had no sense of self without her, and now she was gone. I started having panic attacks, crying. Everywhere. On the Stairmaster, driving, the grocery store.

I hated doing the movie extra work so I got a job as a hostess at a restaurant on Sunset Plaza. I stood outside in the sun, wiped the menus clean, seated people with tears streaming down my cheeks.

One of the busboys asked, "You're not going to kill yourself, are you?"

Writing and Meth
1994

It was a few months after Rilke left when I met Duke and got into crystal meth.

It wasn't Duke who got me all into it, I would have found it anyway, but he was the beginning, the start of me not stopping. I had stopped once before, the one month Rilke and I did it to lose weight. I remember that first time buying it from Athena at the Gentleman's Club, going home and crushing the crystals in tinfoil on the Formica kitchen table.

"You make the beds," I told Rilke. "I'll cut the lines."

I wanted to be in charge of it. She didn't seem to care, but right from the start I cared. I liked the ritual of cutting up the lines, the burn in the nostril, sometimes I would cut her lines with salt so I could have more, but it was never enough.

When we didn't lose weight on it and gave up on the meth diet I never stopped thinking about it, and when Rilke left, that's what I turned to. Meth became my companion.

I also turned to writing. I stopped writing as much around the time I moved in with Cole but something had me back to it when Rilke left. The words kept me company and helped me get through the day. I started to go back through old journals and saw there were stories in those pages. I began transcribing. I'd sit at my stainless steel desk and crush lines next to the keyboard with my library card and I'd type. I escaped the big hours into the ritual of locking myself in my place, curtains drawn, with crystal and words.

People had always asked me if I wanted to be a writer like my dad.

"Definitely not," I'd say.

Even though I felt my dad had led an interesting life I still didn't want the life of a writer for myself, all that time being alone in a room with words and no money. Despite myself I couldn't not write but it was still just something I did for myself, not to be a writer or anything like that.

As the months went on, between going to my dealers and ten-dollar-an-hour jobs, I started taking writing classes at Beverly Hills Adult School. The first one was called 'The Writing Buffet' and only cost thirty dollars for twelve weeks. It was eight older people and me. I liked them and felt safe reading my work aloud. This one eighty-year-old woman rode the blue bus to class every night from Compton. She brought macaroons or homemade corn-bread and read stories all about her life in the South with ten kids, a drunk husband, and a garden. She supported them all cleaning houses and selling batches of jambalaya to a restaurant. She had a spark about her and the way she told her stories about getting on her hands and knees in the garden planting corn and sunflow-ers with her baby on her back and all those little feet of her kids running over what she was trying to plant and bring to life. I held

onto those stories. There was something in her despite her strug-
gles that was alive that I wanted, but it was very far from me and
it would be years before I could begin to see a way towards it.

Dope & Bald Pussies

I'm getting ahead of myself.

Duke was eleven days out of prison when I met him. His family had money, and had found Duke a good lawyer who'd gotten him out of Chino in exchange for twelve months at Chabad Rehab with Rabbi Cohen. I knew right away I needed to stay away. His big prison arms, wifebeater shirt, extra baggy jeans frayed at the cuffs, skull tattoo on one forearm, Lisa written inside a heart on the other, then more blending into each other, bodies entwined, crossbones, and voluptuous women with tiny waists.

It was June. I was eating a Caesar salad at California Chicken Cafe when he walked in. As he ordered at the counter we looked at each other. He sat next to me and gave me his croutons.

Two weeks later I was picking him up at the rehab. I was wearing a hot pink dress, matching string belt cinched at the waist, hair pinned with a crystal clip to one side and clear heels with a black patent leather bow at the toe.

Duke was smoking on the steps waiting for me barefoot, feet wide, big toe black, with three garbage bags of everything he owned beside him. Staring at me as I walked toward him, he flicked his cigarette onto the sidewalk.

"Most beautiful girl I ever saw," he said. "Damn. I gotta get the fuck outta here."

He threw his arms around my waist, lifted me into the air. I looked down at his shoulders. The B and the D of his last name were tattooed across the top of his back where the tank wasn't covering. I wanted my name tattooed on him.

We loaded his garbage bags into my car and went to the Safari Inn. There were three cigarette burns on the polyester bedspread, no shower curtain, and the sink underneath the faucet was stained brown from years of dripping. Duke had meth. He cut a line for me then took the baggie with him into the bathroom and shut the door. I snorted my line through a McDonald's straw, turned on the TV. Girls having sex. I turned it off. Duke was in that bathroom for too long, I realized he was probably shooting up. I wish I didn't snort that line. Later I snorted more.

After three days at Safari Inn, Duke was in a phone booth outside Tony's Liquor Mart. I was in the car with all his belongings. One garbage bag was full of videos. Pulled one out, the title, *Bald Pussies*. I pulled out another, more bald pussies. Maybe I should shave mine.

He was back in the car, he lit a cigarette. His sunglasses were mirrored, I saw my eyes reflected back at me. No blue.

"Cha-ching!" Duke said. "My old dealer's got some stuff. Drive."

It was a few blocks away. I went down a dead-end street. Under the freeway there was a squat, beige house. Duke grabbed the bag of bald porn, I got the other two bags and followed him to a garage behind the house.

Walked in. This converted room had bunkbeds with pink Tinkerbelle sheets. A four-year-old blonde with crooked bangs sat on the bottom bunk rocking a naked Barbie in her lap. There was a dresser, on top of it a dildo and another dildo in a bigger size next to a Cinderella coloring book. I didn't see any crayons.

At the opposite end of the room next to a stove, another white blonde girl, maybe three inches taller, clung onto the long leg of a woman with the same color hair. The woman, who I assumed was the mom, had red blotches on her face.

Grabbing the girl's hair she said, "What did I tell you?"

The little girl was crying, not letting go of her mom's leg. The mom saw us, let go of the girl's hair, picked up a spoon next to the stove and stirred whatever was in the pot.

A couple of days later Duke and me were lying on the grass looking up at the sky in Pan Pacific Park next to the Holocaust Memorial Museum. A helicopter circled overhead, Duke jumped up.

"Fucking fuckheads. Tailing my ass like that."

He took off his wifebeater tank, started waving it around his head like a flag, showing off all his chest tattoos. Orthodox Jews walked by in fur hats and tassels going to pay tribute. Moms pushed strollers and kids threw balls.

"Fuck, come and get me," he yelled. "Down here."

He was pacing and panting. Dogs in the park were barking at him and Duke was barking at that helicopter.

Sex with Duke was good. I didn't want it to be and didn't know how to stop or how it would end but one day, Duke didn't call anymore and there were no more shouts through the mailbox drop. After three days I called LA County Jail.

"Nobody under Duke Brody," the woman said when I got through to booking.

A day later I remembered his aka name. I called again.

"Kasper Brody," I said.

"Booked September 2," the lady said.

Duke. I already knew they were looking for him after he skipped out of rehab. That was the deal, rehab or prison. They got him driving a stolen BMW headed out of Beverly Hills.

It was a Sunday. I wore a white button up and no makeup to that downtown jail. He liked me natural. I stood in the rain with the other women waiting to see their men. They were reading paperbacks and holding umbrellas with elephants on them, fold-up beach chairs, kids hanging onto their legs, babies crying. I thought of my mom visiting Helmet Head in prison and how I had told myself I would never be like my mom with her men and now here I was, standing in the rain on visiting day.

Duke was crying when I saw him behind that thick glass. He wanted to get married and he knew, he knew he was going to do some time. I didn't want to marry him. I knew I was never coming back and that I'd never see him again.

He sent me letters, Chino State Penitentiary, Inmate Number 589745 it read in the left hand corner of the envelope. I didn't read any of them. I was scared if I did, I'd want to visit him again and send him money to put on the books so he could buy cigarettes and Twinkies.

Duke had already spent a couple of years at Chino before we'd met. He'd always talked about how he done and did this and done and did that. How the guys doing life had him hustle for them. He said he put notes up his butt, with messages for guys on the outside to off so-and-so. I didn't ask Duke anything about that. We both kind of understood he'd be back there. And when he did go back, I didn't want mail.

After eight months the letters stopped coming so much. When they did there were drawings of girls, no eyes and arrows in their arms, then no letters.

When Duke went to prison I took all his meth contacts and swore off men. I told myself if I saw a guy I was attracted to I'd cross the street.

I went back to that beige house once. The little blonde girl was sitting on that Tinkerbelle sheet on the bottom bunk like the first time I saw her. Sitting frozen like, holding onto that same naked Barbie. One dildo was on the floor. The mom and the older girl weren't there. I wanted to take her home with me, to protect her.

I looked at her and thought of myself at six. Alone in the park, swinging on a swing in my pink- and white-checkered shorts when the man in the brown car came and took me away.

The little girl looked up at me. I walked over, real gentle. I sat down next to her. We just sat there, quiet, and didn't move, just waited. I don't know what we were waiting for but I didn't want to leave. When darkness came, she put her head in my lap. I put my hand on her forehead, she closed her eyes, I closed mine and curled up next to her. I wanted Rilke to come home from New York.

Let Me See Your Pussy

I got another job as a hostess at Chez Henri in Hollywood. Henri Louis, the owner of the restaurant, enjoyed sharing ecstasy with all his girlfriends. They danced around the restaurant. As I cleaned the menus, Henri would grab me, whirl me into a dance.

"Life is beautiful! Dance little hostess, dance," he'd say, swinging his thin French arms around my waist, then he'd let go and link his arm around another girl. He was not for me.

The tall, blonde Swedish bartender never talked or made eye contact. He was the one for me. He kept his hands busy wiping down the bar and cleaning glasses. He'd hold up a glass, look right through it in my direction, then take the white bar towel and simply polish around the edges. I hoped it was me he saw through the glass at my schoolgirl hostess desk but it never seemed like he did.

One night we worked late. He asked if I needed a ride, I said yes even though I didn't. I sat in his 1970s midnight blue Mercedes. Neither of us talked as he drove west on Venice Boulevard, speeding past motels, McDonalds, Costco, hitting all the green lights. He didn't ask me where I lived. That didn't matter, we were on our way to the water and I wanted to lie next to him on the night sand.

He stopped at Seaway Motel on Lincoln Boulevard. I followed him in and down the hallway to Room 204. 2:30 a.m. We entered. This was not us on the sand lying next to each other. There was a TV playing porn. Two guys were watching it, not paying much attention to the two beautiful girls dancing on the bed in see-through mini-skirts and pink satin push up bras. Holding hands, they jumped from one bed to the other.

I was wearing men's jeans rolled at the cuffs, baggy Nirvana tee-shirt, hair in French braids. My Swede took my hand. This firm, strong hand of his, it was as good as being on the beach with him. He introduced me around. I had to pee. I went to the bathroom, closed the door and sat on the toilet.

The tattooed Asian man opened the door and looked at me, "Let me see your pussy."

"No," I said.

He left. I finished and looked in the mirror. My braids were loose and I looked sleepy, I wished I were thinner like the girls jumping on the bed. I came out. The girls and their guys and the Swede were smoking meth from a glass pipe. They passed it to me.

The Sheetless Bed

I worked at Chez Henri for a couple more months before Henri couldn't pay the bills anymore and it closed down. The Swede moved back to Geneva but before he left he gave me the number of his dealer, Sheila. She had burgundy hair with a hot pink streak that she wore clipped to the side with a rhinestone butterfly that was missing one wing. Sheila lived on Rose Avenue in Venice down the street from Big Lots and Shoe Horn Tavern. She was unreliable.

"I'll be here," she'd say when I called her. "No worries, I'll have the laundry when you get here."

Laundry was her code for meth.

I'd drive over from Hollywood fast on the 10 freeway; if I took too long she wouldn't be there and I'd need to wait at Big Lots Discount store until she came home. I'd look at ninety-nine-cent frames with pictures of men and women sitting on beaches. If I had any meth left I'd bring a frame with a man's arm around a woman, looking at each other, into the bathroom. Sitting on the toilet, I'd take out my baggie that I hid in my wallet, between my library card and my Baskin-Robbins buy-ten-get-one-free card. I'd empty what was left of the crystals onto the glass frame and I'd snort the line on top of the happy couple.

I'd wait a while, then go to Sheila's to see if she was home yet. She always had clothes everywhere, on the table, the floor, the couch. A rack of dresses, slips and royal blue scarves in the kitchen. Sometimes she didn't have the meth when I got there. We'd smoke what was left of her meth from a glass pipe, then I'd wait all night watching her change slips every hour until the delivery came. By the time the meth arrived, her hourglass body had taken on and off all the colors of the rainbow.

One day Sheila said, as she did a lot, "I am going to rehab. I'm telling you, I'm packing up and going. When I go, there's no more Sheila, I'll come back and Sheila, she'll be gone. You won't recognize me."

I had always thought rehab was for rich people. When she said that, I knew I had a problem too, but I wasn't ready to get help or stop. I didn't think I had it in me, and I tried not to think about it.

Sheila never went to rehab. She went to prison. One day I drove over and Sheila and her dresses were gone. There was a pile of dishes in the sink, and a cat I never saw before sleeping on the bed that had no sheets.

Speed at The Yoga Studio

I didn't miss Sheila too long because Duke, before he went away, had introduced me to Roller Girl who made meth with her boyfriend in their backyard. They had three car shells sitting there on broken concrete, attached together in the shape of a bus, a kind of bad trailer that they used to cook it in.

She wore JC Penney jeans and halter-tops, and her nails were always dirty. She shopped her drugs around town on her roller-skates, with her long black ponytail trailing behind.

That boyfriend of hers wore cut-off jean shorts and no shirt. He was extra pasty. His chest hair didn't look right, with patches of it on one side and not on the other, and his belly button didn't look right either; the doctor didn't cut his bellybutton cord close enough, and it stuck out a good couple inches. He was nice enough, though. Offered me lemonade and meth.

Before Duke went away to prison, he'd told me about the boyfriend: "He wants to be me. Always been jealous of me. I've known him for years. I can just see it in those eyes of his, sizing me up and wanting to be me. He's got respect for all the time I did."

I wasn't sure about that, but I didn't tell him.

Sometimes Roller Girl and her boyfriend delivered the meth to me. By this time I had quit hostessing and gotten a job at a yoga studio on Third Street in between Benito's Tacos and Tony the Taylor. My job was to collect the money and welcome the girls; they wore burgundy leggings and oiled their wrists with frankincense and patchouli. By the time they got to Downward Facing Dog, I had slid fifty dollars into my pocket, and by the time they were in Salutation To The Sun, I was outside dialing Roller Girl's number for a delivery.

I'd pace and look over the railing as I waited for the boyfriend's blue pickup truck with its skull and crossbones on the back window. The two of them usually arrived during meditation, when the ladies were sitting cross-legged with thumb to index finger, breathing in, breathing out.

We did the exchange outside of Tony's Tailor, below the yoga studio. I'd run down the steps to get my stuff, then back up the steps, into the studio, and into the bathroom where I'd crush crystals in between two pages of Wellness Today.

When I went to their place, the meth was always there. Sometimes when it was cooking, I wrote in my journal or read a book on their bed. By that time I was taking night classes at UCLA Extension; I was enrolled in Major and Minor English, and American Women Authors. (I loved that class.) I remember one night being at Roller Girl's while they cooked, and reading *Ethan Frome*. I wasn't a fast reader but that book, I couldn't put it down. The meth took an extra-long time that night. Being with them was better than being home alone.

Corn on The Cob and Porn
1996

A year later, Roller Girl and her boyfriend moved to the desert. They introduced me to Eddie who became my new dealer. He was a year out of prison, fifty, tall, thin with dyed black hair and green eyes. I was attracted to him and went over to his place a lot. One night, it was about two in the morning, Eddy was eating corn on the cob with my feet in his lap. He was watching porn; two skinny guys in yellow hard hats were taking turns having sex with a girl bent over a metal ladder. Her hands and shiny red nails held onto the sides as she looked over her shoulder, licking her lips.

Eddy's corn looked good. There was a knock on the door.

"Who's it?" Eddy asked.

"Kasper, asshole."

Eddy stood up, opened the door.

"Let's vacate," Kasper said. "Tiger's got it."

Tiger was in that band that sang "Eye of the Tiger" in *Rocky*. I don't know what his real name was.

I turned off the TV, didn't want to leave that girl hanging

there. The three of us got in Kasper's orange lowrider truck. I sat in the middle. Jesus on a cross, hung from the rear view mirror swinging back and forth as the truck rattled on the way to get meth. I hoped to get a fat baggie so it could last me the week.

Kasper drove crazy. My knee kept hitting the gear, Jesus hit the window, and Eddy flicked corn from his teeth. Why was I attracted to him? He was a bad dad, dyed his gray hair black, went to prison, and had sex with Kasper's girl, Lisa.

I didn't know what Eddy noticed besides feet. I knew I wasn't special to him, not like this nineteen-year old he liked. Her mom had overdosed in the parking lot at Marshalls. The girl was chunky, never smiled, but her toes lined up all perfect. That's what Eddy liked.

Kasper parked on a street lined with short trees and one-story houses with white curtains, pebble walkways, and tin mailboxes with red flags. 1508. Kasper, Eddy, and I walked up the pathway. It was January. A rotten Halloween pumpkin was set on the porch to greet us with its eyes and mouth sagging downward. Eddy knocked on the door. No answer. I stared down at Kasper's toenails in his flip-flops. How did they get so clean and well cut? The pumpkin was sneering at me. I wanted to kick it, to get my meth and go home.

Tiger opened the door. He wore the same low-armpit kind of tank he had on last time. His skinny loose arms and all that pale skin hung there. They made me sad. To think ten years ago, he was famous and singing with girls screaming for him. The lights, the stage. Airplanes with pretty stewardesses and extra peanuts. Now, now he had those flabby arms and a dead pumpkin.

Tiger's wife was in the kitchen rustling through plastic bags. Crumple, crumple. She was spreading them out on the faded yellow linoleum floor in her bunny-printed muumuu dress, with about a hundred extra pounds behind those bunnies. I didn't think people who did meth could manage to eat so many cookies. She flattened and folded one plastic bag after another, stuffing them into paper bags from Vons and Ralphs.

On the glass coffee table in the living room there were beautiful, fat white lines of meth. Tiger nodded to us. Me, Kasper, and Eddy, we were already on our knees with straws up our noses. Snort, snort. I thought of pigeons flying in for breadcrumbs on the street.

Tiger was hanging from his chin-up bar in the doorway separating the kitchen from the living room. He didn't try to pull up, just hung there. I did another line, went into the kitchen, and started folding up plastic bags with that wife of his.

Cartwheels and Clumsy Squirrels

Eddie started to put my whole foot in his mouth. Then we were kissing and he was on top of me. His house painter's bucket, next to the fake aqua leather couch, was filled with little bottles of sparkling nail polish. The TV was on with more porn; he always had porn on.

Kasper was there and we were waiting for his girl, Lisa, to bring the meth. Eddie began painting my toenails dark purple. After the big toe had dried he sucked on it as he slid his hand down his pants. Kasper sat there with his pants down, watching me with my toe in Eddie's mouth, and I was looking at Kasper's name tattooed on his white belly. Spelled with a K, I'd thought it was with a C. Under the S in his name he tugged on his dick, it was soft and pale. He kept pulling on it but it stayed limp in his hand even though he was watching Eddie and I who were now on the floor. I wondered why the meth was this late and what colors Eddie would paint the rest of my toes after sex.

The meth didn't arrive, and Eddie didn't finish my toes.

He told me, "You go to Lisa's grandparents place, she'll be there with the meth."

I had been to Lisa's before. I drove over but she wasn't there, just her grandparents who she lived with. They let me wait in Lisa's little girl's room. A unicorn with stuffing coming out of its horn was leaned up against the urn of her dad's ashes under a heavy metal poster. The little girl's name, Libby, was blue-crayoned on the wall in the arc of a rainbow. They called her Lib. Lavender jeans, pink socks, underwear with strawberries on them and puzzle pieces were scattered on the floor. The single bed in her long, narrow room was level with the window. I sat on Lib's unmade bed. I pictured Lib rolling out of that window into the dry brush outside with that stuffed unicorn in her arms, and then rolling farther, far away from that house, the meth, the urn, and her grandpa who I just knew undressed her.

Lib walked in with her stringy hair in her face. Her feet were bare, scabs on her knees and shins. I wanted her mom, Lisa, to come back with a hundred dollar 'skull baggie'. I also wanted to bathe Lib, wrap her up in a blanket and tell her she was loved and everything was going to be alright.

But I knew it wouldn't be. Lib looked at me.

"You're not my mommy's friend," she said.

I looked out the window. Lisa was home now, doing cartwheels outside. She was upside-down with her feet bare reaching to the sky, her hands on the dead grass. She did two more cartwheels.

I wondered if Lisa brought the meth. Suddenly Lib started screaming. I ran out to the lawn, past a faded flamingo on a rusty stem that was stuck in the ground. The flamingo reminded me of men in motels in Florida.

Lib was still screaming and Lisa, still at her cartwheels. A dog was on the lawn now too, barking. It had patchy hair and barked like some barking chords were missing.

"I don't got the meth." Lisa shrugged, like what's the big deal.

"It'll be here soon, good stuff. None of that bunk-ass shit."

I was thirsty. I walked down the block to Taco Bell to the drive through.

"Need to be in a car to order in this window, lady." The girl in the square window had one gold tooth and wore an orange headset.

Inside I ordered a coke, and a plate of refried beans with salsa. The beans were cold and made me really hungry. I ordered another with tacos and a burrito. The burrito reminded me of this stripper at The Wild Goose with small hard nipples, no boobs, but an ass the guys liked. She knew it. Every night she'd eat a big burrito at a table by the stage. She'd take her time, eating, watching girls swing from the pole, hanging upside down. Was she still stripping? I didn't know.

I ate my burrito as I watched a clumsy squirrel try to climb a tree outside the window. The squirrel couldn't get up that tree right. I felt like helping that squirrel. I thought of Lib, tears came. Maybe I wouldn't go back to her house. It made me too sad seeing her, like I was supposed to do something to help her, but I didn't know what.

Tears dropped into my second plate of cold beans. My forehead felt tight and I was tired. I pushed the food aside and put my head down on the orange plastic table. I wanted to curl up right there, or maybe under the tree with the clumsy squirrel. I raised my head, looked out the window, I didn't see the squirrel but Lib was there alone right outside on a banana-seat bicycle with pink spokes. I walked outside. She didn't see me. I didn't want to scare her, in slow motion I walked toward her. She was riding that banana bike slow. I walked to the side, letting her see me first and she did. She stopped pedaling. I stopped walking.

She stuck her tongue out at me. Bare feet to the pedals, and those pink spokes circled round and round and then faster and faster and she was gone.

I couldn't go back. Not to the grandparents' house with the cartwheels, that urn, the unicorn, and Lib.

I walked up the street to get my car. I didn't turn my head toward that house. Key in the ignition, foot on the pedal, I left.

I was on the 10 freeway headed west, not to Hollywood where I lived. I took the Sepulveda exit, passed Vons and the 76 Station to Eddy's. His black truck with the raised wheels and a *Playboy* decal on his back window was still parked outside the flat beige building. He lived in apartment one, bottom floor, nearest the street.

I knocked on the metal screen door. No answer, I stood there. The door opened and Eddy with his tall skinny body dressed in black was there, his white arms tattooed with cartoon women with little waists and big boobs, and I felt better.

I fell asleep on his aqua couch while he painted my toes. I didn't care what color or if he put my feet in his mouth while I slept. I just wanted to sleep and not be alone.

Writing

When Rilke got married and moved to New York we didn't talk much. That was our style, just like when we were kids. We wrote letters sometimes but we didn't talk on the phone in-between the times we saw each other every summer just like now.

"I'm pregnant," she called to tell me.

I'd always wanted her to have a baby, and it's what she always wanted. I still didn't want to have a baby or get married even though people kept telling me that would change. I thought of the giving birth, the nightmares I had as a kid after the man in the brown car took me away, the sleepwalking into my dad and Alina's room. The drugs helped me not think about all that, but I wondered if I would have wanted a baby if there never was a man in a brown car.

I also always thought I wouldn't want to have a baby unless I could be a good mom. When I took care of Alex, I didn't think I was very good at it. Not a good mom to him. I always had this feeling even as a young girl, that I wouldn't be the kind of mom I would want to be until I was fifty and it was too late.

I heard people say it's selfish to not have a child. I didn't see it that way. What seemed selfish was bringing a being into this world and not taking care of it. And there were already so many unwanted babies to begin with.

And getting married, it just never made any sense to me. I felt it would just make things go wrong between me and whoever I was with.

Rilke also said New York was hard.

"I'm not so sure about raising a baby here," she said.

Maybe she would move back to LA.

"Are you seeing anyone?" Rilke asked.

After Duke, I hadn't been with anybody except that one night on the floor with Eddy. I was scared after Duke of making another bad choice. I felt certain that I'd be attracted to a guy that wouldn't be good for me, and that I would have to quit meth before I met someone, because no good guy would want a meth girl. For about two years, whenever I met a guy I was drawn to, I walked away. Until I met Ricardo.

I told Rilke all about the classes I was taking at UCLA Extension. I had accumulated a number of credits by this time.

"I'm in a writing workshop now," I told her.

"What are you going to do with all those credits?"

I wasn't really sure.

Up until now, between my dad having his new life with Miriam and me being on my own, he and I hadn't seen each other much since I had graduated high school. During the time I started taking classes at UCLA Extension, my dad was asked to read a poem at the 75th anniversary of The Iowa Writers Workshop. He asked if I would go with him. I'll never forget the three days spent with him on the same campus he had attended and taught at years ago. At the opening ceremony he read a poem he had written there in the 50s.

Iowa

What a strange happiness.
Sixty poets have gone off drunken, weeping into the hills,
I among them.
There is no one of us who is not a fool.
What is to be found there?
What is the point in this?
Someone scrawls six lines and says them.
What a strange happiness.

I met writers I'd looked up to for many years, and students immersed in the program.

"Could you see yourself going to college here?" my dad had asked.

He had always wanted me to get a degree but getting accepted, the money, being an older student. I couldn't imagine it.

"No, I can't," I told him.

A part of me was envious, though, with the life of a student, learning and engaging on levels that I imagined to be fulfilling.

Coming home from that experience I started attending workshops on different writers he was giving every eight weeks. I loved the classes I was taking in LA and I knew, despite the self-destructive choices I had been making, that I craved a connection with others. This had always come through stories, the one thing that made me feel less alone in the world.

Every other month I'd visit my dad and sit with writers in a circle in his living room and look out the floor-to-ceiling windows at the towering redwoods as we discussed the lives and poetry of Sylvia Plath, Robert Frost, James Baldwin and many others. I remembered my dad telling me about hosting a dinner party for Baldwin. I was finally becoming interested in my dad's writing life.

It was in those poetry workshops and classes at UCLA Extension that I had a sense of nourishment. One of the teachers I had at the extension had encouraged me to start submitting my work to literary journals. I set a goal for myself. I would accumulate one hundred rejection letters. Only I liked to use the word motivation letters. I received many, and it inspired me to send more work out. Often I would receive comments from an editor, not always positive. One editor wrote a two-page letter to me listing all the problems she had with the piece. It was a story about my mother. I continued to send it out. That story ended up being my first to get accepted into an anthology. By the end of the year I had reached my goal. One hundred motivation letters, a number of acceptance letters too. I recognized the discipline that had been instilled in me perhaps through the ballet lessons growing up, going off to dance class every day while most of my classmates hung out in their free time.

After a year, my dad asked if I would like to be his assistant at a memoir retreat he was giving at Esalen. For a week I was immersed in the craft of memoir during the day and sitting in the hot springs nestled into the Big Sur cliffs at night. Every day the writers gathered, sitting cross-legged beneath the skylights of the wood cabin with rays of light shining upon us. My dad would instruct us to close our eyes.

"Imagine yourself in your first childhood home," he said. "I want you to really see it, to be present with the images, the scents, the textures that come."

Then he would ring the gentle bell of the cymbals and we would open our eyes and bring pen to paper.

"For twenty minutes, let your hand move across the page with whatever comes. No stopping, no censorship."

Heads down, pen in hand, all eight of us spreading memories across the page as the Big Sur waves crashed against the cliffs. I saw myself in a sepia-toned picture that was taken when I was six. Hair in two braids that were coming apart, a well-worn velvet dress, the hem on one side unstitched, tied around my neck a key attached to a dirty ribbon and a wool bonnet, rubber boots with bare legs. I was leaning up against the outside wall of my dad's outdoor writing studio, his rusted Raleigh bicycle propped up next to me. I was looking into the camera face-on, not smiling. I looked like the saddest girl in the world. As this picture came to mind, tears ran down my face and blurred the words I was forming onto the page.

I listened to the other writers share what they had written. The rawness and immediacy of what they read aloud inspired me. Being at that retreat, it touched a seed within me that felt like it had been there since I was a child; I was surrounded and naturally drawn into the poetry of words. But to write? To be a writer? That meant I would need to face the lonely, frightening hours of sitting with myself. My deepest desire was one day maybe that would be possible. But I was nowhere near that day.

Ricardo's Unshared Dream
1999

Under the Echo Park summer sun brown and pale, long-haired beauties dressed in hand-me-downs. Slender hands with amber and turquoise rings picked through heaps of clothes. Some stood naked so long, I feared my boyfriend Ricardo would look through the window at them. Him full of lust. Me full of jealousy.

I loved Ricardo. He liked Bob Dylan, old movies, Somerset Maugham and Bukowski. But Ricardo wrote poetry, and the one thing I said growing up is I'm not having any poet. No money. Constant revisions.

I met Ricardo at a party in Echo Park. I was sitting on a red velvet couch. He came over.

"I write poetry," he said.

"That's too bad." I got up. Walked away.

The next morning he tipped his 1950s hat and bowed good-bye. That summer I moved in with him.

❁

It was the night with the curtains when I knew I was going to be with Ricardo. It was the second time I had been to his place. I bought him blue curtains. I drove down Sunset, passed Hollywood, Los Feliz, Silver Lake, and turned at the mural of women in red-and-orange skirts making tamales on Echo Park Boulevard.

I was wearing dark red leather boots, a rose-colored dress, hair loose and curly. 1568 Palmer Street. I knocked on his door.

"Come in, my lady," he said, opening the door, taking my hand and kissing it. He was wearing a blue-and-green flannel shirt, dark blue jeans, and black corduroy slippers. "Welcome to my chamber."

Bare bulbs cast ungenerous light on his one-bedroom bungalow. Brick-brown living room, harsh self-portraits, a fireplace stacked with books, and flowered sheets trying to be curtains.

"I'm not sure about these." He looked at the blue real curtains. "Not really me," he said. "I am making us paprika popcorn."

I followed him to the narrow kitchen that divided the back bedroom from the living room. Peeling yellow linoleum floor. Brown bananas on top of a mini fridge. He poured olive oil into a big pot. We watched the blueish flame, waited for the oil to sizzle. He poured in the kernels, put on the lid. He used the cuffs of his flannel shirt as pot handles as he shook popping corn over the flame.

On a small worn-out couch, cushions covered with that flower curtain material, our thighs touched. We watched part of a movie, held hands, ate the orange popcorn. It was spicy and good.

I thought it was time for me to go. I wanted him to tell me it wasn't. He didn't, he stood up and kissed me. I heard raindrops on the roof. Walking up the hill to my car I didn't see one star through the rain. I thought I might never see him and his corduroy slippers again. I just sat in my car. Me and the rain. I started to cry. Walked down the hill, knocked on his door.

"I forgot my curtains," I said.

"Silly girl." He smiled.

We lay in his bed in our clothes under a gray wool blanket. He curled up close to me on his side. Put his arms around me. Next morning he said, "Let's hang the curtains."

Here's the rule I decided:

"Weekends together, one week day," I told Ricardo.

Sometimes I broke that rule. I'd drive over in the middle of the night. Knock on his door.

"What are you doing here?" He'd open the door naked.

I liked listening to his breathing, kissing the back of his neck, waking to the coo of pigeons mating on the beam.

It was about eight months in when Ricardo said, "I think you should move in with me."

"I don't think that's a good idea," I told him. "Seems we like each other a whole lot, why would we want to ruin that?"

I also thought I couldn't live with him without him finding out about the drugs. But five months later I moved in with him in Echo Park. He never did find out about the drugs. It's hard to believe, and when I tell people they can't believe it either. It must have worked for him on some level, both of us in our own worlds, him with his poetry and guitar, watching the Lakers. Me in the back room, writing, color-coding the closet, or gardening.

"You really like to keep that closet organized," Ricardo would say. "And you sure got a thing for being in the garden."

I don't like gardening or organizing, but on meth it was very interesting.

Every morning Ricardo would go off to deliver flowers, and I'd go off to work at the yoga studio. Sometimes I wondered if Beth, Celeste, and Simone were still stripping, and if they weren't, how did they make their money?

After work, Ricardo and I would walk along the trail through Elysian Park all the way to the LA River. Sitting there around sunset one night Ricardo told me his dream:

"I want to live in the mountains and write and grow tomatoes. I'll come up with songs and poems and won't deliver flowers anymore. One day I'm going to do that."

He talked about that a lot. I can't remember if I even had a dream, but living on a mountain wasn't it. I told him so but that didn't get in the way.

Love and Ricardo in Echo Park

Every weekday morning Ricardo delivered flowers through Echo Park, with its taco stands, burrito trucks, and carts with cayenne-peppered cucumbers, pineapple and mango. The skinny man pushed his *helado* cart up the hill; it was painted orange with two wheels and a bell, one wheel about to fall off. I'd run out, wanting ice cream. He was too fast. Ringing that bell up the hill, never looking back to see if anyone wanted a frozen strawberry bar.

On Saturday mornings red watermelon trucks rumbled down the street. Sometimes watermelons fell out and we'd run into the street and get them and have watermelon parties in our courtyard with the neighbors' flamenco-singing father. We'd watch him sing and dance with his big nose and skinny legs. We'd spit watermelon seeds in the fire pit.

Then Ricardo and I would walk across the street to Lupita's Market. Lupita had black hair to her waist with strands of silver coming through. Her sister visited every summer from Mexico. They sat on yellow milk crates. Spanish soap operas played on a black-and-white TV on another crate. A wire coat hanger for an antennae. Dollar Store Jesus candles underneath where the milk used to be. We put tortillas on credit.

"Anything else?" Lupita asked. "Red pepper, banana?"

We also picked rolls from a big plastic bin with a red top, raisin bran discolored from sitting on the shelf too long in the sun, cornflakes in the wrong aisle next to canned beans with rusty tops. By winter, Lupita's sister would be gone.

Lupita had chickens in the back of her market, fenced in. She used to have a rooster, too. That rooster seemed like it got confused, crowing earlier and earlier. Then he started losing his crow. Sounded more like a cackle than a crow. Like it had a cold or something. One day there was no more crowing.

"A coyote must have got him, or maybe he moved away," Ricardo said.

Our neighbor Lucero the bungalow queen collected rent, so she got a discount. She lived top center of the five bungalows, by the courtyard in the middle. Ricardo wrote, sitting on our hand-me-down love sofa with one leg missing. A Balzac book in its place. Lucero walked by in a pirate costume, another day as a bird with purple feathers coming out of her head. A flapper girl or a silk kimono, nothing underneath, for days when she was nude modeling.

One day, Lucero's flamenco-singer father came to visit from Spain and never left. He'd stand on the red picnic bench in the courtyard singing flamenco at three in the morning. Dingy white boxers, skinny bare legs, cigarette between two of his bony pale fingers.

Pink flowers bloomed in the summer, reaching out beyond the crooked wooden fence away from the courtyard. Francesco twisted each flower back in so it faced the courtyard, away from my front window and door. I twisted the flowers the other way. Back and forth we'd go.

For Ricardo's birthday I blew up silver-and-green balloons. Left heart-shaped notes on his pillow and between his guitar strings. Then I'd put Revlon candy apple lipstick on, make kiss marks on the cracked bathroom mirror.

We walked through Elysian Park to his birthday party. Piñatas hung from trees. More balloons, yellow and purple tied to branches. Carne asada on the park grill. Little brown-bellied kids ran with sticks in between walnut trees and balloons, trying to hit the swaying piñata. Back and forth, back and forth. Families spread out around checkered tablecloths on the grass.

It was Monday morning. I was wearing my see-through white nightgown with pink embroidery cut above the knee. Standing outside the mud-brown front door, barefoot on tiptoes, I kissed Ricardo goodbye on his warm neck.

"Have a good day at work," I said.

Ricardo didn't go home for naps like some of the other flower delivery drivers. I watched him start up his 1998 stick-shift Honda and he was gone. Gone to deliver those flowers.

Lucero walked up wearing a pink boa around her neck, sunflower dress and a cowboy hat with a peacock feather sticking out of it.

"Can I borrow a cup of rice?" she asked.

"There's some in the cupboard," I said.

I went to Lupita's Market, bought lettuce and green chili tamales for dinner. On the way to Lupita's I saw that Rita, my friend, had posted on all the trees that her cat Chewy was missing.

Later, I set the table, lit a candle and stood outside to greet Ricardo when he came home. Bamboo chimes hung over my head from a hook screwed into the green awning above the door.

We'd found the chimes on top of a garbage bin. Two chimes missing, it slanted heavier on one side. I'd never heard it make music with the wind. Walgreens had stainless steel ones with purple butterflies on sale for five ninety-nine. I'd walked in two times to buy those chimes and I'd stolen jungle-green eyeliner the first, bought family-size Red Vines the second.

Ricardo parked his car, walked up the steps. He had orange lilies in his arms for me. We heard noise behind us and looked in the street. Three Echo Park coyotes had Chewy.

We took the lilies and walked over to Rita's.

It was a Saturday morning. I made thin crepes burnt along the edges with Canadian maple syrup the way Ricardo liked. A blue star-shaped mirror was set on the chipped windowpane above the full sink. It was my turn to do the dishes. Outside the window red-and-green Christmas lights sagged in a slope tied between two bamboo shoots. It was July. Purple flowers grew between the cracks in the cement. Three garbage bins to the right, rusted weight bench to the left, a blue-and-white striped dishcloth hanging on the bar. There was a yellow stain on it. The stain depressed me. I wondered how people kept white things white and how they took down Christmas lights after Christmas.

Ricardo walked up behind me, kissed my neck. He was naked except for his old-man black corduroy slippers. His thighs, big; Mexican skin, pale. He didn't look like his six brothers and sisters. When he was grumpy, he'd tell me, "I must've been adopted."

I didn't know what that had to do with being grumpy, and I knew he wasn't adopted. I had seen a picture of his dad, whom he'd never known, a black-and-white of his dad taken before Ricardo was born, standing in high-waist pants next to his white

Chevy. Looked just like him. He had a full head of floppy hair and sleepy potato-chip eyes just like Ricardo's, the eyes I liked to kiss and lick, salty and warm.

I poured syrup on the crepes, walked outside, picked a purple flower and stuck it in the middle of the crepe. Rolled up a fork in a paper towel with dinosaur print and set it on the wooden table in the living room. I watched Ricardo eat while listening to the angry Saturday morning preacher at the church next door. I promised myself I wouldn't do speed that day. I'd be normal: shower, dress, make the bed, take a walk and talk to the neighbors.

An hour later Ricardo was showering and I was in the Murphy bed closet squatting on the floor crunching lines of crystal meth in between two pages of *The Sun Also Rises*. I reached up into the pocket of my red coat that hung on a pink plastic hanger and I took out a red-and-white striped straw that had been cut at the tip. I stuck it up my nose, leaned down into Hemingway's words, and snorted the white crystals. I felt the burn of the nose, eyes watering, a drip down my throat.

The Typewriter

"I don't know what to get Ricardo for Christmas," I told my dad on the phone.

"Go to the Hadassah's, find a great old hardback book, maybe a first edition."

Ricardo loved books. The fireplace filled with them, the shelves beneath the living room windows, books stacked on the floor next to the couch.

I drove over to Fairfax, stopped at Canter's Deli to sit at the counter on one of the red swivel chairs. Ordered matzo ball soup, ate pickles and marzipan in the shape of a miniature pig from the bakery on my way out. I nibbled the head off as I walked down Fairfax, past an old Jewish lady in a black raincoat pushing a bundle buggy with plastic bags of rolls, and oranges tied to the handles. I walked into a thrift store with a blue-and-white star in the window. Musty. Smelled like my mom's closet in Florida. I sneezed. I was always sneezing in Florida when I visited my mom during the summer. Racks of dresses, slacks, mended wool sweaters, shoes worn at the sole. Ricardo liked me in thrift store clothes.

"Vintage," he said.

I didn't think 80s was vintage, but I didn't tell him that. I tried on a pair of shoes. One heel was higher than the other. Put my flats back on. Walked up the stairs stacked on the sides with books. Old comics, paperback romance novels with covers of women with long flowing hair mounted on horses. Some with men mounted on the horse, the woman's arm wrapped around his waist. Other covers with dark-haired men off in the distance, but all the covers had horses, men, and women. I hoped upstairs would lead me to Balzac.

The room at the top of the stairs was small with a low ceiling. Along one wall: glasses, plates, baskets, a blender, fans. Books piled high in the corner. Next to an eggbeater was a typewriter. Royal, like the one my dad had when I was a kid. He still had it. I leaned down. The keys were dusty, the ribbon gone. I placed two fingers on the keys. *Click, click.* I thought of my dad. The earliest sound I remembered. And mockingbirds. (I used to say owls until Ricardo, he told me, "That's no owl, silly. That's what you call a California mockingbird.")

Ricardo knew lots of stuff like that. Whenever we went for walks, he could name the trees, birds, and bushes. Bushes that you'd never even think to look at, bushes that didn't look like anything at all, just a bunch of dry twigs all squashed together. You put a good name on an ugly bush and it gives that thing some dignity.

Ricardo knew a whole lot about typewriters, too. There was no doubt this one here, this was the gift. It was a heavy thing, though. I had to carry that Royal two blocks. Felt like ten, but I knew he would like it and I wanted to hear the keys make poetry and bring me back to the good part of childhood.

Doll Girl

Lucero and her nude model friends were having a party in the courtyard. Girls toasted marshmallows, hair loose, braless in sheer blouses; they sat around the fire watching Ricardo bring new logs.

A beautiful dark-haired girl with porcelain skin, black lashes that curled up, and red lips sat next to me.

"You look just like a doll," Ricardo said to her.

She smiled, licked sticky sugar from her fingers. My face, it was too hot next to the pit. I inched back out of the circle. Doll Girl and Ricardo looked at each other. She got up, walked to the red picnic bench. Yellow sundress tied behind her neck, the pleats accentuated her hips as she turned around, her thick hair hung far down her bare back. I watched Ricardo watch her. I imagined them together on that mountain he told me about when we first met. The one he said one day he was going to move to and quit his job. He still talked about that a lot, and had gone down to working four days a week since I had met him.

"Can't stand working for the man," he'd say.

I felt the same, but the mountain still didn't sound good to me, and besides, he never mentioned me when he talked about that mountain in the first place.

I went inside our home, sat on the couch, turned on the TV and flipped through channels on mute. No lights on. The images from the TV cast a blueish glow to the room, then dark, back to blue. I could hear the crackling of the fire. Laughter. I got up, looked through the window, a bush blocked my view. I didn't want to see. Not Lucero with her model friends, or anything else. Tomorrow I would go to the yoga studio to work, make ten dollars an hour, bring home eighty.

How much did Doll Girl make, sitting nude while people drew her in charcoal? Ricardo walked in.

"Come back out, Santa."

"I don't want to. Looking at you and that girl, I just keep picturing you two in bed together."

"Don't be silly. You're the girl for me."

"Well, it's in my head. I'm going to Chango for a muffin."

"If you think a blueberry muffin will help." He kissed the top of my head, went back outside to the girls.

I walked down the hill, past Magic Gas, crossed Echo Park Boulevard to Chango next to Lupita's. Lupita was sweeping the sidewalk in front of her store. She was wearing a red dress that I hadn't seen before, her gray hair in a single braid. Maybe she had a date later.

"*Buenos noches. Donde esta Ricardo?*"

"*Casa,*" I said, following her in.

I couldn't go to Chango without buying something from Lupita. Felt like I was cheating on her if I didn't. I picked out an over-ripe avocado from a basket next to the register, a few baby plantains.

Then I went to Chango and stood in line. A tall, young, dark-haired man was working behind the counter.

"What can I get you?" he asked.

I pointed to a pastry in the glass display. He reached for it, a leather cuff on his wrist. His hands looked strong, I imagined him pinning me against the wall in the backroom of the coffee shop, kissing me.

"Anything else?" he asked, not looking at me.

His attention was on the girl behind me. She had blonde hair cut pageboy style, red lips, leather jacket. I wanted him to look at me. If he did I'd feel better about Ricardo and that Doll Girl. I decided I'd go back to Chango looking better next time, wearing red lipstick. Smile, but maybe he didn't like girls that smiled. I looked at the girl behind me. She was pouty, looked unhappy. I should look unhappy, I was unhappy. I didn't know what I was doing with my life, I couldn't imagine stopping the meth, and tomorrow I'd be sitting at a yoga studio and I didn't even like yoga and I was with a poet who had a dream that wasn't my dream. I wanted a dream, too.

I walked back up the hill to home. The pastry tasted stale. I threw it in a bush. Ricardo was at his desk, typing. The girls were still outside.

"Why aren't you out there?" I asked.

"I got bored," he said.

I wondered what he was writing. A poem about her?

Helpless Feet

Ricardo and I were naked in the kitchen. He opened a yellow tin with "Ibarra" in red lettering and put two chocolate wedges in a pot on the stove. We watched the chocolate melt. Ricardo added milk, waited for it to warm, poured it into two mugs without handles.

Sitting in bed, pillows propped up behind our backs, we leaned against the wall, hands warm around the mugs. I looked at his bare feet, the hair on his toes. Touched my foot with his.

"Your feet make me sad," he said.

"Why?" I asked.

"Sometimes when you sleep, one foot hangs over the bed. It looks so helpless. I get that foot back into bed and cover it up."

I wondered if he thought I might walk out.

"I like the way your toes line up," I said. "Kind of like piano keys."

We looked at his feet as we drank our Mexican hot chocolate, not too sweet, tasted like smoky cinnamon bark.

"Two years ago you didn't even know me," he said. "What did you think of me that night we met?"

"You looked green to me, but I thought you were interesting. I liked that you were in the kitchen with me eating carrot cake while everyone else was drinking in the living room."

"And you thought I was Italian," he said. "Someone made mushroom cookies, I ate two, I think that's why I looked green."

"What did you think of me?"

"I thought you were weird. I liked you right off. And you did your own thing, going into another whole room, sitting there reading a book."

We set the cups on a wooden chair next to the bed. Turned off the light, got under the wool blanket, pulled it up to our chins.

"Itchy," I said.

He got up. I could see the outline of his body, his strong thighs. He called them baseball thighs.

"All the great players have them," he told me.

He walked into the closet, shook out a flowered sheet, the one that used to hang in the window until I brought over the blue curtains. I kicked the wool blanket to the floor, he spread the sheet on top of me, threw the blanket back on, got into bed. We pulled the covers over our heads.

I could feel the warmth of his breath. With the tips of my nails, lightly, I drew circles, zigzags up his back to the nape of his neck, kissed his ears, and we fell asleep.

Sunday morning we rode our bikes to Brite Spot on Sunset Boulevard across the street from Edendale library. I wore black-netted tights, lace-up boots, flared mini skirt, tee-shirt without a bra. Ricardo, a flannel, Dickies, and sandals. He held my hand as we walked in.

"Let's sit at the booth," I said.

There were lots of couples, women with unbrushed hair, unshaven men in beanies. Brite Spot was the East Side's version of Swingers, where girls don't have black roots coming through bleached hair or wear tights with no tears. We ordered scrambled eggs, bacon, sourdough toast with marmalade, and drank free refills of weak coffee in orange mugs.

After, we rode our bikes home from Brite Spot. Me on my black cruiser that Ricardo bought me from Sully's Used Wheels on Crenshaw. Bikes everywhere, all from the police yard.

"Unwanted bikes," Ricardo told me. "Police don't know what to do with them when they arrest someone on a bike. Cuffed and put in the back of the police car, they gotta bring it to a yard of arrested bikes that get auctioned off, and guys like Sully show up."

I wondered what the guy who owned my bike was booked for, or girl. Ricardo found his bike leaned up against a lamppost on his street. That lamppost was where just about the whole neighborhood brought things they didn't want. Someone always picked up whatever was set there. Sometimes they brought it back, like the shoes I had set out. Next day they were gone, a week later they were back. Ricardo's lamppost bike was missing the chain, but he could fix just about anything.

"I'm what you call a Mr. Fix it," he told me.

I liked that about him.

We rode by Echo Park Lake with the paddle boats, locusts, palm trees. Passed the fruit man with his cart of sliced cucumbers and mangoes with cayenne pepper. Deliah's Bakery, *pan de huevos, cremas frescas, empanadas* set on trays in the window.

When we got home Ricardo sat at the slanted wood table in

front of his Royal typewriter. I sat on the love sofa with a red knitted blanket covering the worn cushions with my journal in my lap.

"Let's buy a new couch," I said.

"It's quiet time."

I watched him *click, click* on the typewriter. I thought of my Dad, picked up my pen, opened my journal and looked at the empty white page. What should I write?

Dirt Angels

One day Ricardo came home and said, "What you're looking at here is a man who is claiming back his freedom. I've cut back to three days a week delivering those flowers."

I didn't know what to make of that. I was still working at the yoga studio five days a week.

"What about our plan to save money?"

"Save for what?" he asked.

"A nicer place."

"All I hear in that is being trapped in a job I don't like."

We had been through this before. I didn't say one more word about it that night. I didn't want to try and take whatever it was he was feeling about being a freer man away from him, but it gave me thoughts about how I could be a freer woman.

On his days off Ricardo started to build his dream, beam by beam behind his sister's house on a hill in Mount Washington. She had a forest of a backyard.

"It's a little tricky building on a slope," he told me before going to the lumberyard.

He went every day, driving off with one plank at a time sticking out of his Honda.

Ten months later he said, "It's really coming along. Let's have a barbecue there."

I hadn't been to see it yet.

We went to the market in Eagle Rock. Cowbells tied to the doorknob rang as we walked in, a thin man with a straw hat sat on a stool playing the banjo near the register, a woman wearing a potato-print apron and a blue kerchief tied around her hair swept the floor.

"*Buenos días*," she said.

It was warm inside, smelled like fish.

"*¿Cómo estás?*" Ricardo asked.

"*Bien, bien.*"

We picked out four ears of corn and a mango, walked to the meat counter. A man with a black mustache and a bloodstained white apron wiped sweat from his upper lip with his forearm. "*Caliente.*"

"*Sí.*" Ricardo looked over the meat. "Quarter pound *carne asada, por favor.*"

We went back to his sister's house, walked down the hill behind it. Stood in the frame of his studio that was smaller than our bedroom.

"This here is where my desk will be," Ricardo said. "Right in front of the window so I can see out while I write. A hot plate on that ledge there, for making tea and boiling rice and beans. And right there, I'll have a bed."

"You're going to sleep here?"

"Well yeah. This will be my cave, my own writing retreat."

"What if I want to spend the night?" I asked. "Looks like a

birdhouse for one. That bed area is only big enough for a single mattress."

"There's not going to be any mattress in here. I got a yoga mat and a sleeping bag."

That dream he had, the one he'd shared with me when we first met about living on a mountain together and writing, there was no room for me in that dream. Even if I never wanted to be a part of it in the first place, it didn't feel too good seeing this was a place for one. It was strange though, I also had this good kind of feeling that he wasn't going to do something he didn't want to do and resent me. Like live in a nicer place and work a job he didn't like.

Outside, we'd set a hibachi in the dirt.

"What are we thinking?" He opened a bag of charcoal. "It must be ninety degrees."

We shucked the leaves off the corn, unwrapped the red meat, and set the food on the grill. Ricardo took off his shirt and sandals, walked over to a hose, turned it on and watered his feet. I took off my shoes, stood close to him, our feet cool and wet together.

I thought of what he'd told me when I moved in with him. "We'll grow old together. You'll have long gray hair. We'll go to the forest and make a bed of leaves on the ground and lay down and have sex under the trees."

The sun was going down. We ate, laid on the ground, looked up at the sky.

"What are you thinking?"

"I wish we were laying in the snow so we could make snow angels," I said.

Ricardo moved his arms and legs from straight position, then up, down. I copied him.

"Dirt angels," he said.

With our arms turned into wings we fluttered, looking up at the purple blue sky. We rose, backsides covered in dirt, looked at our angels, and went home.

Moving Out

2003

I still loved Ricardo when I moved out, and he loved me, but I didn't want to live with the mice in the oven, the peeling linoleum living room floors, and Lucero's drunken father singing in his boxers in the courtyard. Ricardo, he was working less and less, and spending more time on his mountain writing poetry and growing tomatoes.

I started looking for a new place to live while Ricardo continued building his cave. I saw a lot of ugly studio apartments.

'Adorable one-room with patio in Silver Lake.'

It ended up being one room with a mini fridge on the floor, mustard carpet that had cigarette burns, and a sliding glass door that opened to the patio that was really a slab of concrete, three feet wide and so high you couldn't see over, even with a ladder.

'Charming, quaint, hardwood floor bachelor in the heart of everything on Western Avenue.'

It was an old twelve-story brick building in between Korean BBQ and Bargain Bin.

"Everyone who lives here is very quiet and keeps to themselves," the manager told me. "No animals or late-night parties. Building is kept secure with a camera in front, and maintenance is always on hand."

I followed the manager down a hallway, past the flickering florescent light bulb and up the stairwell that smelled like cigarette smoke to the fifth floor.

"Elevator works," he said. "But good for the legs, the stairs are."

He unlocked the first door on his left. The room was a bright box with a view of Chung's Auto supply. I thought of Ricardo driving to Mt. Washington with his wood. Maybe he could make his studio big enough for two, or build one next to his for me.

"Nine hundred, utilities included," the man said.

I pictured my bed and paintings, wood desk. I heard a baby crying. I felt like crying, all those ugly homes. I couldn't live on Western Avenue, and I wasn't going to live on a mountain, away from everything. Maybe I'd call the place with the patio. I went home to Ricardo.

The next day I went with him as he brought another plank of wood over to his hill. Next to the barbecue was a row of dirt he fertilized.

"For the tomatoes and lettuce," he said. "I just got to keep the raccoons away."

I looked at the fertilizer. Didn't look like any place I'd ever seen anything grow in but Ricardo, he made things grow that you'd just never knew could. That row of dirt would make him a salad one day.

I found a large room with French doors, pink-tiled bathroom, high ceilings in Hancock Park. No kitchen, but a private overgrown backyard and private entrance from the main house. The landlord, a skinny German woman, lived up front with her thirty-eight-year-old son.

That first month I didn't spend one night there. I'd drive over from Ricardo's, look at my new home, and drive back to Ricardo's.

Mom, Meth, and College

My mom was visiting for a week after Ricardo and I broke up. But he was still my friend, and that meant a whole lot to me because it never seemed right not ever being in contact with Cole after I left, and I didn't want to end something that way again. By this time, my mom had met a new man, Peter. They had met back in college in Ann Arbor. Forty years later, after Peter's wife died and my mom's lifeguard boyfriend left her, my mom and Peter reunited.

"Your mother was supposed to come visit me in Connecticut for the summer," he said. "Before she got here UPS boxes came to my door. The boxes kept coming and she never left. I'm a lucky man. When I met her in college, your mother was the most beautiful, not to mention smart. We were all in love with her."

Peter was the nicest man I ever met. He was not like the other boyfriends my mom had. I was still working at the yoga studio when they came to visit. One night we were at dinner and

I was telling them that with all those classes I had been taking, I had accumulated a year's worth of college credit with a 4.0 at UCLA Extension.

"You already know you come from a smart family," my mom said when I told her about the classes. "Little Grandma and your great-grandma being lawyers, your aunt Lydia a judge, and God knows what it took for me to go to Architecture school. I was the only girl in my class and your grandpa, one of the best surgeons in New York."

I don't know how it happened or why, but during that visit my mom and Peter said if I wanted to go back to college, they would pay for it. I couldn't believe it, and I also couldn't believe that since my mom was with Peter she was more like a mom. She was a mom. She asked questions like how was I doing, and she told me how proud she was of me. I didn't know what she could be proud about, and I also didn't know how she couldn't tell I was on drugs, just like Ricardo didn't know. It didn't seem like any of the jobs I had had known either, because I never got fired, and that didn't make any sense to me. Maybe everyone did know and they just didn't say anything.

My mom had never had any money before, but when my grandparents died, she had some inheritance money to help pay for it, and Peter was also helping. I started Antioch that fall.

It would take me a year to finish my BA. I majored in Creative Writing and took all the classes I was scared to take, like Statistics and Biology. My classmates were also older adults going back to school. The classes were small, and there were tutors that I met with for math, and an advisor to guide me through. There were a lot of times I wasn't sure I could do it, that I wasn't smart enough. I thought about all the jobs I had had, from stripping to chopping potatoes. I kept at it. I couldn't do the kind of work I had been doing. I was thirty-two. And for the first time in my life, my mom felt really there. I didn't know how long it would last, but I felt like the luckiest girl. I knew it was a luxury to go back to school, to have it paid for. I wanted to do well.

"You could be a CEO, I can picture you now," my mom said.

I wasn't sure about the CEO, but I wanted to please my mom and get a good enough job after I graduated for her to continue to be there.

I want to be able to say her being there fixed everything, or at least some things, like the drugs. But it didn't.

I continued to use when I went back to college. I thought I couldn't do it without the meth. My plan was to quit when I graduated. In statistics, I remember the teacher talking to me after class.

"Your notes are good enough to give to a substitute teacher. But really, you don't need to type out the equations."

I couldn't not type them out. It was the meth. I would spend hours at home working on a paper. Foucault vs. Rorty. Blue Whales. Attachment Theory. During that time I started writing articles for a neighborhood newspaper covering the Third Street area for thirty-dollars an article. I wrote twenty-three. From doggy wear stores and Indian Cuisine to Baskin-Robbins. I turned the articles into stories about the owners. I received credit for these articles for an independent studies class. Was able to graduate early.

There was one woman, Bala Moontaro, who sat next to me in Child Development. She had white gray curly hair, full body and next to her on the desk she always had a beautiful glass bottle of water with mint leaves in it. It was the mint leaves that made me want to be like her. On break I would go to the bathroom, crush and snort a few lines off the top of the metal toilet paper dispenser, come back, and there would be Bala and her pure water. I always wanted to be a woman like her. The kind of woman who goes to the farmer's market and buys yellow gerberas or peonies for herself and puts organic basil in her salad. I looked at Bala and thought I'd never be like her or like the old lady at Beverly Hills adult school with her spark and her garden. It made me sad. I did more meth and tried not to think about the woman I wouldn't become. But maybe after college I would get better, I'd get a normal job and stop the drugs and be able to sit with myself and write at night.

I enrolled in one course Bala had encouraged me to check out. I was reluctant, but it was three units and I thought it would be relatively easy. It was a four day silent meditation retreat at Mount Baldy Zen Center. The whole time, I was on crystal meth. My cabin was next to the gong. Every morning at four one of the monks rang the gong. All the retreaters walked up the hill to the Zendo with wool blankets wrapped around them for the first of five meditations each day. There was no eye contact allowed. Walking up that hill you had to be careful not to look at anyone. I tried my best to keep my gaze to their feet or straight in front of me at the trees and the sky but one time I looked right at one of the monks. I felt bad because eye contact was considered stealing, some sort of distraction, and seeking attention from another person instead of going inward. I felt bad about doing the crystal meth too.

I had my meth all worked out. Before going to the Zendo I'd snort it on the floor of my cabin with a picture of the Buddha smiling on the wall in front of me. By day two I had to take his picture down and turn it around. I'd get high again before lunch and not again for the whole rest of the day so I could sleep at night. That was real hard, but I did it. I ate, too. All that grain and tofu they served. I must have looked healthier after those four days with eating and sleeping. When I got back to LA, Bala said something looked different about me. That I had color in my face. It didn't last long, though. I went right back to doing meth all day, not sleeping, and eating maybe a pack of strawberry Twizzlers for the day. I never meditated again, not ever. Those four days felt more like three weeks. After the retreat, we were assigned to write a fifteen-page paper. I chose and became deeply engaged in writing about The Four Noble Truths in Buddhism, despite being far from living them.

The hardest class I took was Attachment Theory.

"It is crucial for a child to form an attachment to his or her mother in the early years," the teacher read aloud. "The effects of not doing so are devastating for a child."

Reading about it, watching films about it, I saw myself as a child in those children. I felt things I didn't want to feel. Sometimes I missed class. I wondered what kind of woman I would be like if my mom hadn't left. Maybe I would have chosen basil over meth, made choices that weren't destructive, if I had formed a sense of self. But my mom was here now, and she was paying for me to sit in this class.

Office Girl

I finished college and I hadn't done meth in two and a half weeks. I slept for the first three days, and then I couldn't stop eating. Family packs of black licorice, granola, hamburgers, and burritos.

I hadn't planned on trying to quit, but the last time I talked to Lisa, she'd said, "All my connections are getting busted right now." I kept trying to call her but she wasn't returning any of my calls and I couldn't get a hold of any of my old dealers. I drove by all their houses. Eddie's black truck wasn't there anymore, Roller Girl's place was all boarded up, Sheila was probably still in prison, Chez Henri where the Swede worked had been turned into a mattress store, and I couldn't remember exactly where Tiger lived but I drove around and around his neighborhood looking for that dead pumpkin on his porch that had probably rotted away a long time ago.

Two or three times a week I went on job interviews. At thirty-three it was my first time applying for jobs that required a degree.

"Look sharp," my mom said. "Go out and buy yourself a crisp

suit, and wear Little Grandma's NYU law school pendants. And bring the silk handkerchief she gave you. Pull it out of your purse to dab your nose during the interview. That will show you have class."

I wore one of the suits I had saved from my days with the Madame. I had kept it in the back of the closet in a plastic suit bag, the kind with the zipper on the side that always reminded me of a corpse bag. I bought an alarm clock and stockings like the ones my mom had worn when she had worked at Burdines. I kept hearing her voice when I looked at all the varieties at the department store.

"The worst two years of my life."

I wore glasses, tied my hair back, and went on seventeen job interviews, and I was called back four times for an administrative assistant position in the dean's office at a law school.

The law school, Southwestern Law, had bought the old Bullocks Wilshire building in Koreatown as an extension of the campus. The Bullocks Wilshire used to be a department store where all the famous people shopped in the 30s and 40s.

On the day of the fourth interview I pulled up to the kiosk.

"I'm here for an appointment with Dean James," I told the security guard.

"Keep your sunshine, young lady," he said, opening the gate.

I parked and looked up at the six-story art deco building. I walked towards the two-hundred-foot tower. The bronze had tarnished to green, the outside entrance was marble. Mae West and Lauren Bacall used to drive up to the carport with the mural ceiling. I was buzzed through the big brass doors.

"I'm Ms. Yamamoto," a woman said, extending her hand. "I am the dean's executive secretary."

Her nails were French manicured, black hair straight and shiny; she wore a crisp black suit with a high-collared cream blouse.

"Right this way," she said, pressing the elevator button with the cuff of her sleeve.

We stepped inside, took the elevator to the fifth floor, then crossed the hall into an office that lead to an adjoining room. She knocked on the door. No answer.

"This was Mr. Bullock's master suite," she said. "Many nights it was said he slept here. There's still a Murphy bed in the wall. There's a dressing room and master bathroom with a heated towel rack."

She knocked again. An elegant man opened the door.

"Ms. Sward is here when you are ready," she said.

He was a short man but seemed taller because he moved quickly and was well-built. He had a kind face, pale blue eyes. He extended his warm hand.

"I am Dean James. Please have a seat in front of the fireplace."

Ms. Yamamoto shut the door behind her. The room was four times the size of where I lived. I sat up straight on the edge of the couch. Hands folded in my lap, knees pressed together. He sat in a brown leather chair opposite me. I faced glass doors that led to the balcony. Beyond the pots of geraniums and ivy I could see all of downtown. I knew I would not get this job.

"This is just a formality," Dean James said.

I looked at the rosewood desk to the left of the fireplace.

"That was Mr. Bullock's," he said.

"I've never seen a bigger desk."

"It was built during Prohibition." He smiled and looked around the room. "There are many hidden compartments. You will find there is a lot hidden in this building."

I took out my handkerchief from my purse. Dabbed my nose, delicate.

"I understand that at this point you have a good idea of what this job entails." He crossed his ankles, and I saw the tip of a monogram on his black socks. "I'm interested, how is it you came to see yourself working at a law school?"

I didn't want to say, "Well, I needed a job."

"I'd like to work in an environment where I'll be learning. That would be so rewarding to me, because to tell you the truth, my grandmother and great-grandmother were lawyers, and my aunt was a judge. Theirs was the first female family law office in New York."

"Impressive lineage," he said, leaning forward. "I see you're wearing NYU law school pendants."

"They belonged to my grandmothers. They all went there. I have a picture I can show you of my grandmothers with Eleanor Roosevelt."

I blushed. I wanted this job. I couldn't bear the thought of going on any more job interviews. There was a knock on the door, Ms. Yamamoto cracked it open. "Your next appointment is here."

I went home and wrote Dean James a thank-you card. I had read that's what you are supposed to do after interviews.

It had been a week and I hadn't heard from the law school. I was washing my white button-up shirt in the bathroom sink with plans to go on an interview for a nine-dollar-an-hour tutor position at an Elementary School. The phone rang. It was HR from Southwestern.

"We would like to offer you the position of Dean's Office Assistant. When can you start?"

The Bra Department and Eleanor Roosevelt

Day one at Southwestern Law School.

"Ms. Sunshine is back," the guard said. "I am not surprised."

I took the elevator to the fifth floor where I met with Ms. Yamamoto.

"This office was once part of the bra department," Ms. Yamamoto told me. "There is no door separating our desks from each other."

The walls were dark paneled wood, on one side was a glass case filled with illustrated history books of the Bullocks Wilshire.

"This is a historical landmark," Ms. Yamamoto reminded me as she unlocked the case. "Everything has been preserved." She handed me a book. "I will give you a tour later. The desk in the corner is your area. Take some time to settle in."

There was one window above my desk with a view to the hallway leading to the elevator. On the wall, next to my window, was a framed picture of Carole Lombard posing next to a live mannequin in a bullet bra. Below Carole I placed the picture of Little Grandma, Great Grandma and Aunt Marion with Eleanor Roosevelt.

"That picture was taken when your Aunt became a judge," my mom had said. "At the ceremony for your aunt I went to the Hadassah and bought a suit. I will send it to you."

I was wearing that suit on my first day. It was a little small; my body felt stiff in it and I wanted to take it off. I ask Ms. Yamamoto how long she'd been working there.

"Twenty years," she said. "Most of the administration has."

I looked out my window with the view to the elevator. I didn't know how I would make it to Friday. It was very hard to keep up with everything Ms. Yamamoto was trying to teach me. I had gone to the bathroom to call Rilke in New York.

"I can't do this," I told her. "I'm not smart enough."

"Of course you are," she said. "It's just your first day. Like the first day at the strip club, you didn't think you could do that."

"But I don't know how to work a nine-to-five job."

"You can do it. We just never saw anyone going to an office growing up, except Mom's miserable time at Burdines. That wasn't our world."

I pictured my mom back then putting on her light-blue skirt suit every morning. I sat on the lid of the toilet not wanting to come out, thinking how bad I wanted meth. It would make it easier. Through the crack in the stall I watched the law school girls with their textbooks and high ponytails washing their hands, looking all smart.

At lunch I went to The Tea Room. It looked just like it did in the old pictures. Pale green tiles, cactus-etched copper grating, long windows looking out at the Hollywood Hills, salmon drapes tied back with gold braided cords. Next to the board of specials for the day, a life-sized photograph of Lucille Ball sitting at one of the tables wearing white gloves drinking tea.

Pigeon Music

I had been working at the law school for two months and I still hadn't done meth. I thought about it all the time. The hours were so long and I knew the meth would make the days go by faster. I called Lisa a couple times but hung up. I had to stay stopped.

From the outside you wouldn't know how scary quiet the pretty art deco building was, but walk inside and it was eerie. Only pigeons hung out in the tower. I heard them fluttering through the walls with a curious rattle, I never didn't hear it. The pigeons were a soundtrack to Ms. Yamamoto's stories about her dead husband. Every morning as I drank too much coffee and ate lots of oatmeal cookies, she would tell me another story. Then I would try and escape into the back room to make photocopies. I always jammed the photocopy machine. It only destroyed paper when I used it.

At eleven, she would hand me the key to the faculty lounge.

"You need to distribute the mail."

I didn't mean to be a mail person. I'd take the stairwell down to the fourth floor. I wanted to keep going and walk right out, but then I would have to find another job.

I'd tip toe by Mr. Boden's office to get to the mail lounge. He taught Criminal Law. If he saw me, he followed. I wished he didn't like me. He was not handsome and his name was Don. Sounded like one of my mother's men.

In the faculty lounge, there were big windows that looked out at other office buildings with views of trees. I thought that if my desk was outside with trees I would be a better worker. There was a kitchen for the law professors in the lounge where there was always leftover birthday cake. I cut myself a slice every time. If someone walked in, I slipped the cake into one of the cubby-holes where the mail went.

A Metal Arm

The only part I liked about my job was the dean, but he had to travel a lot. When he wasn't out of town I would go to The Tea Room and get him black coffee. No cream or sugar. I always liked it when a man drank it black. Cream and sugar seemed womanly to me.

One time when I brought him coffee, he said, "I read one of your father's books. One day you'll write a book. Make sure you bring me a signed copy."

I couldn't imagine that ever happening, but I didn't tell him that. The dean researched and conducted many interviews of lawyers and how they came to choose their chosen practice such as Wills and Trusts, Immigration, or Entertainment Law. Part of my job was transcribing his research and interviews. He asked very good questions. Transcribing was like reading a story. Sometimes I imagined the dean was interviewing me. I wondered what my story would sound like.

He also had me edit the professors' summer grant research proposals. I would have thought that they'd edit their own proposals.

"Whatever the length of their proposal," he told me, "it needs to be summarized into five pages for the board to review."

Mr. Boden's proposal ended up being the one I found most worthy and engaging to read. He wanted a grant to research wrongfully incarcerated prisoners. Despite my desire to avoid him, I still hoped he would get the grant, and I wasn't sure he would because the stats seemed incomplete and hard to follow. I still stayed away from him in the professors' lounge, though.

Sometimes I wrote my own stories when I had spare time at work, and sometimes even when I didn't have spare time. I was always worried that Ms. Yamamoto would walk behind me when I was writing, but I did it anyway. One day I got some very good news from Ms. Yamamoto.

"Next week we will have privacy screens for our computers. Confidentiality is essential."

I wasn't sure what anyone would be looking for, but once we got them I didn't worry about her checking to see what I was doing anymore. I also found out some not-good news.

Doc, the security guard asked me, "How's Ms. Yamamoto doing with her MS?"

I knew nothing about it and thought it must be coming on slow. After that I tried to be much more patient with her telling stories about her dead husband.

While I was working at SWL I only went on one coffee date. A student with a metal arm had come in to talk to the dean. His arm bent at the elbow and his fingers were like big tweezers.

He was tall, had strong legs, black eyelashes that looked like he curled them, and I had a crush on him. His name was Nate.

Two days after he came in Ms. Yamamoto told me that Nate said I was beautiful. I was very surprised. I waited for him to come in again but he never did. A couple of months later, though, I was in line at The Tea Room for coffee and Nate came up behind me.

"I'm sure you're very busy in the Dean's Office, but maybe you and I could grab lunch one day," he said.

We made a plan for lunch in the Tea Room the next day. I remember he ate a Chinese chicken salad with his left hand, his tweezer hand rested on the table.

"I never expected to go to law school," he said.

"I understand that, I never thought I'd work in a law school."

"What did you do before this job?"

I didn't know what to say.

"Well, I just kind of had odd jobs. I'm going to get some more water, do you want some?"

When I was with Ricardo, I had always worried he'd find out about my past. He never did. I wondered if I would be able to hide it again? Part of me didn't even want to hide it anymore. All those secrets with Ricardo, I hoped I would be able to be honest and not so ashamed in my next relationship.

Nate didn't ask anything more about work when I got back, but he did ask for my number. He never called it.

My Way Too Long Stretch Inside the Well-Preserved Bullocks Wilshire with the San Quentin Guard

I had stayed away from meth for so long that I really thought it was over. That I'd stay clean. But one of Lisa's connections must have gotten released from prison because she called, and within twenty-four hours I couldn't get out of the bathroom stall.

The fourth floor one at SWL had the best privacy, because people didn't always see me go in. Sometimes there were students studying on the lounge couch. I'd walk into the bathroom, and by the time I came out they'd be gone, or at least I hoped they would be. I'd spend my whole lunch break in there sitting on the toilet seat. I'd balance a professionalism textbook on my knees, take out the bag of crystals from my wallet, crush a few lines between the pages. If someone was in the bathroom I'd flush, crush, and lean over the book in case they walked by the stall and saw me through the crack in the door. I flushed again when I sniffed through the straw and then pick, pick, pick. I couldn't stop picking at my arms and face. I'd take out a compact mirror and pluck the hairs above my upper lip and chin, then crush another line.

I started to bring a change of shoes so if someone came in

they wouldn't recognize my feet. I'd switch from the pair I walked in with into black flats.

I had been working there two years when I sat with the dean in front of his unlit fire in his office as he read my employee evaluation out loud.

"A ten for being open to critique, not defensive, and for listening," he said. "Excellent." He paused. "Low on efficiency, example stated; not returning in due time after distributing mail, going to the library, or after checking in on a mock trial."

"I am sorry about the low efficiency," I said.

"That is not how I view the work you do for me," he said.

Once a year there was a silent auction scholarship fundraiser. Jesse Jackson was the featured guest the first year I attended. He spoke about the importance of raising money for minorities. After that, the ballroom was opened for bidding. The ballroom had high ceilings painted with mosaics, white columns and velvet drapes. It used to be the gown department. One of the trustees with a red face asked me if I liked wine.

"If you do I'll bid high for it and get it for you," he said.

The only wine I ever bought was Two-Buck Chuck from Trader Joe's, and I could hardly finish a glass the rare time I had any at a party. I never had a taste for alcohol. The trustee wrote six hundred in the bidding column, three quarters of my rent. I tried to imagine kissing him.

"He has a reputation with the ladies," Ms. Yamamoto told me.

I wondered what it would be like to be with a man who had

money. Instead I'd fallen in love with a poor poet who delivered flowers. I could never pretend to love a man that I didn't love.

Graduation was at the Shrine downtown where the music awards were held. The whole time I stared at the back of Bob Dylan's head. What I thought was his head, anyway. His son was graduating. I imagined how proud Dylan must be, and I hoped that when my mom and dad were at my college graduation they had been proud, too. I wondered if they would still be if I quit my job? The doors at the SWL ceremony opened extra early for him to take his seat so he wouldn't disrupt the ceremony.

"He's the one with the beanie on," someone told me. "In the middle there."

I thought he was such an animated man, nodding his head the whole time, looking, shaking it. I was very interested in all his movements. Hand coming up to his beard, stroking it, arm around the woman beside him.

Later someone told me he was sitting in the front row. I couldn't believe I'd spent two hours analyzing not Dylan's head, but I forgot about him soon enough and went back to thinking about how I didn't want to disappoint my parents.

A faculty member had a wife who'd recently gotten out of Betty Ford. She had a drinking problem. He had a picture of her on his desk, about fifteen years younger than him, bushy blonde hair. I imagined he would be a very nice man to be married to. I was standing by his desk the first time I met her. She walked in, tossing her Pashmina over her shoulder.

"We're going to the opera tonight," she told me.

I'd never been to the opera. I wondered if she'd be thinking of drinking while she was sitting there in the Walt Disney Concert Hall.

One day, Ms. Yamamoto was at a doctor's appointment. I sat at her desk trying not to hang up on anyone that was on hold. I always got confused with all the red blinking lights. I hadn't been able to reach Lisa in six days, it was horrible when she disappeared. I couldn't stop eating, and all I wanted to do was sleep. I found Adderall in Ms. Yamamoto's drawer, the prescription date was old. I took two and felt terrible about stealing her medication with her MS. I put the pills back and called Lisa again, left another message, then I opened the drawer again where the Adderall was and took one.

A week after the opera the faculty member's wife went back to Betty Ford, and that same day, Lisa called me after disappearing for two weeks.

"Meet you in the bra aisle at twelve," she said.

I took the 10 freeway to Ross on the Westside, a few blocks from the cutlery company she worked for. I had so many forks. It took me forty minutes to get there. I worried she wouldn't show up, but there she was in the 34C section with her red hair and black-painted eyes.

"This is extra good stuff," Lisa told me as she slipped the baggy into my hand.

I'd go straight to the change room to do a couple lines. The thing about meeting at Ross was I had a real hard time getting out of there, even though I hated the place. I'd tell myself, leave, go back to work, but that speed made everything look so interesting. The salt and pepper shakers, underwear, curtains. Especially curtains, I had a thing for them. If I thought they were too expensive I'd switch the price tags.

I called into work on my way back.

"Locked my keys and phone in the car."

I said that a lot. It was another job I hadn't been fired from, I didn't understand why.

Sometimes the speed did help me to be a good worker. The hours would go by fast, I'd get busy, very busy. Making file folders, organizing, making more file folder labels, editing summer research grant proposals and editing them again.

I was transferred out of the dungeon building. I couldn't believe my good fortune.

"We're relocating you to a room in the Westmoreland building," Ms. Yamamoto told me.

I didn't ask why. Just packed up my files and moved out. Westmoreland was a 1970s concrete block. From the outside you wouldn't know it, just like you wouldn't know how dreary Bullocks was until you went inside, but it had life in there. Students, windows, and I could wander around anytime I wanted since I had my own office. Best of all, no dead husband stories, or at least not so many. I missed the dean, but I still saw him when I checked in for my assignments.

I started to walk off campus every day. I wondered if the security guard, Doc, saw me on the cameras when I left. If he did, he never said anything. I'd walk down Vermont to Ralphs, the deli man knew me.

"Quarter pound of turkey?" he'd ask.

Most the time that was my diet, turkey and apples. I didn't need to eat hardly anything else all day with the meth. I'd walk back down Vermont eating my meat out of a plastic bag, sit on the curb outside Koreatown Bowling, tear open a mustard packet with my teeth, squirt it on. Vermont was an unattractive street. KFC, gas station, Walgreens. I worked on stories in my head on those walks, then I'd come back to my desk at SWL and write it all down. I tried taking the prettier side streets but the stories didn't come.

I also wondered if Doc, who called me Sunshine, could see me on his surveillance cameras when I sat on the stairwell. I hid there on my way to another office a lot and cried. It was very hard to work from nine to six.

"I used to be a prison guard at San Quentin," he told me. "You know, I'm working on a children's book during my down time. I'll bring you a copy. It's about a caterpillar that loses its way home and never becomes a butterfly. I know you will become a butterfly one day."

Then he pulled me to him and kissed me. He was actually pretty handsome, but I didn't know what to make of that and pulled back.

"I'm sorry," he said. "I just had to, before your sunshine goes away."

Somerset

It was just before Labor Day when Rilke called and said she was moving back to LA. By Halloween she was back with her husband Jonas and their baby. I loved being an aunt. I cried the first time I saw Somerset and started babysitting whenever I could, pushing him in his stroller through Pan Pacific Park, watching him crawl around the playground in the sand and try and get in the swing. Up until then, whenever I saw a swing and park, I felt cold inside and saw the man in the brown car and in the swing as a six-year-old in my pink- and white-checkered shorts. But being with Somerset there, I felt like I was creating new memories. On the days when I knew I'd be babysitting I didn't do meth. Above anything else, doing it when I was with him or any child, that was not okay.

I hated my office job more and more. It wasn't long before I went down to part-time and started looking for another job. Rilke drove with me down Wilshire Boulevard as we thought about what kind of a job I could do next, and where.

"That building doesn't look so depressing," Rilke would say. "You could work in some doctor's office, or a dermatologist."

A twenty-eight-story slab of concrete with small windows.

Tears would come to my eyes as I pictured myself in one of the offices. Rilke understood. We drove into Beverly Hills.

"What about in a nice hotel as a front desk person?" she asked.

I looked at the Beverly Hilton and the ivy growing up the wall and the big hedges. I remembered being in a room at that very hotel years earlier when I was Lana with a hairless man in his seventies who just wanted to look at me naked.

"Maybe I should just keep my job," I said. "That's what people do, they work whether they like their job or not."

Foot Fetish Work
2006

Going down to part time, I was hardly able to pay my rent, and even with a husband, Rilke was having trouble with money too. She had been personal training and teaching Pilates in New York but didn't have many clients now that she was back in LA. We started coming up with ideas for jobs that we could do together.

"If we can just make $100 a day," Rilke said.

"We could exist on that. Even $400 a week."

"In New York, I did a little foot fetish work. All I had to do was let some guy lick my feet."

"And Jonas, he was okay with that?" I asked.

"You know how he grew up, his mom being a dominatrix and all. Pretty unconventional. It wasn't like I was having sex. You know, I heard dominatrix teams do well."

Rilke's mother-in-law, Vea, who worked as an accountant in New York, had fifteen years of experience being a dominatrix. She was six feet tall: a beautiful Jamaican woman with high cheekbones, elegant neck, slanted brown eyes, and long black lashes.

"I can give you all the advice you need," Vea told us over the speakerphone from her work. "When I first started I took a workshop in the Village. Actually, a seminar. And I learned how to tie up balls with rope and chain. You girls will make a good team. My boss is here. I've got to go."

Over the next few days we decided to try it. It would be like when we used to work together as Claudia and Lola, only ten years later. Vea wrote an ad for us to post online.

"You need to have a lesson on how to be a dominatrix," Vea told us.

Jonas told us that we could call his pot connection, Ruby, who was LA's number one dom for seven years. Ruby was forty-one and had twin twenty-year-old boys, owned a duplex near Paramount Studios, and was going back to get her degree in business management at Cal State. In the meantime, she was selling pot and mushrooms to earn a living.

Ruby came over. She had burgundy hair and smelled of cigarettes and patchouli. We offered her iced tea and took notes at Rilke's kitchen table as she talked to us:

- *No sex between a dom and a client.*
- *Most common, foot and leg worship.*
- *They never want to be really pleased.*
- *The goal is you want to shatter male ego.*
- *Work on verbal humiliation. 'I've seen bigger dicks than yours.'*
- *They are alpha males but they don't want the control they have.*
- *You've got to learn a proper spanking.*
- *Get a nasty attitude.*
- *Do not use pussy names like 'honey' or 'sweetie'. That is submissive. Tell them, 'Stupid, ugly man, get on your knees.'*

Before Ruby left, she said, "You girls will need equipment.

Leather, garters, plastic handcuffs, whips. Call me anytime if you have any questions."

We decided to wait until we met and interviewed a potential client before we bought any equipment. I figured it would be okay because I'd be with Rilke. Neither of us were totally sure we wanted to do this, but we thought we would give it a try.

The Interview at Swingers

Our first client interview was a married lawyer from Manhattan Beach. Rilke and I got fire-engine-red pedicures, wore black stilettos, black tanks, cleavage bras, and smoky gray eyeshadow. She picked me up at 9:20 a.m. Somerset was in the baby seat in the back, we dropped him off at the babysitter then headed to Swingers, a diner in Hollywood. Our 'slave boy' was sitting outside Swingers in his BMW. In his picture he had hair and looked less schlubby.

We chose a booth in the back away from the jukebox and people.

"What can I get you?" the waitress asked Rilke.

"He'll have a warm banana nut muffin."

I could hardly say a word the whole time and let Rilke do all the talking. I don't remember what she said, only him saying, "I'm looking for one session a week. I very much love my wife and kids, but I need to be humiliated."

I just kind of stared at this man's warm muffin and tried to look mean by squinting my eyes like how I imagined a dominatrix would be.

When we left, Rilke looked at me. "What the hell happened to you? You cowered in the corner shaking like a reindeer. We were supposed to be dominatrixes."

"I got nervous."

"Nervous? You were a wreck."

As we drove to pick Somerset up I said, "I guess this isn't going to work."

"Well, apparently not. Besides, he's not going to call us."

But he did, asking when we could meet up for a session.

We never called him back.

"We still have to work together," Rilke said. "Let's think."

"What are our assets? What can we both do?" I asked.

"Well, you can do secretarial work, and I can personal train and cook."

We decided to try it and went back to her place, took photos of me in a sexy-but-not-too-sexy secretary's outfit and Rilke in her workout gear. We posted an ad on Craigslist. 'Sister Services All in One: Personal Assistant/Personal Trainer/Cook'. Then we went to pick up Somerset from the babysitter.

The next day we got one response back.

"You both are stunning," a man wrote. "But I already found my assistants. Would you ladies be interested in the adult arena?"

We didn't respond, and again that Monday I went back to my office job and wondered how I was going to make it through the day and how I was going to pay my rent.

Sugar Daddies

A month later, Rilke's mother-in-law came to visit at Thanksgiving. At dinner she told me,

"You have soft eyes. Many men should take care of you. This cranberry sauce could be better."

She helped herself to seconds.

"When I was your age I placed my first ad in *The Village Voice*. Honey, I had so many men. I'm sixty and still have one of my men after all these years. Tuna. He's a good man. He comes over once a week and I handcuff and whip him, and he pays my rent. I'd marry him if he wasn't already married."

"I can't do the dominatrix thing," I told her. "I don't have it in me."

"Honey, there are other ways you can get a man to help you. It is too much for you to do all on your own."

I agreed, it was too much for me. And continuing to try and do it on my own, that would take a capable type of woman. Far from who I felt I was, or ever could be.

"I see you in an exclusive situation where you have one or two men helping you who you see regularly, like me with Tuna.

He's a nice man and the agreement is I see him once a week. I'll tell you honey, that man has been good to me all these years. I whip him and he loves my cooking, so if he's hungry I make dinner for him and he goes home."

I could quit my job. No more fluorescent lights or looking at the clock. I'd work being with a man once a week, I'd have my own Tuna, like Vea. I'd have all that time to write, and I could really try to quit meth, and everything would be so much better. But I still wasn't sure. What would I tell my mom? She had invested all that money into my college, and so had Peter. How could I quit this job that they thought was good?

The Orthodox Sugar Daddy

The weekend after Thanksgiving, I was in the file room at SWL crying on the phone to Rilke about not having rent.

Vea was still in town.

"Tell her not to worry," I heard her say in the background. "I'm cooking curried chicken for dinner. We'll think of something."

"Maybe I should try the sugar daddy thing," I said.

I left work early.

"Now sit by me." Vea handed me a bowl of curried chicken. "You're going to do just fine. I wrote an ad for you. We just need a headless body shot of you."

This is what she wrote:

I am tall (5' 7"), slender, elegant, classy, and in my thirties. I am not a pro—just someone who needs regular financial help on a monthly basis. I am looking for an exclusive relationship with a mature, preferably married man who is well-established and very generous. Someone who wants a no-strings, regular long-term relationship. You would find me passionate, uninhibit-

ed, sensuous, and completely trustworthy. So, if you are interest-
ed, please contact me so we can talk and decide when and where
to meet for a drink to see if we like each other.

I found a picture of myself posing in heels and red garters. We cropped my head out of the picture and posted the ad on Craigslist.

Over the next few days I got many replies.

"Want to play on this," one guy wrote with a snapshot of his dick.

Another wanted to meet that night in a motel. I decided I didn't do motels. Then a guy wrote that he was handsome, young and could give me a hundred dollars. I wrote back, "If you think a hundred dollars is a lot of money, you're too young."

Then there was the man who described himself as a shorter Richard Gere. Or maybe he didn't say shorter, but he was.

"Meet me at the outside lounge at Chateau Marmont," he said.

I wore a backless black dress, high heels, and pink lip gloss. It was chilly that night and my legs were bare and cool. Thirty minutes earlier I had been at home in my royal blue sweats and red socks with reindeer on them. I hadn't even met him yet, and I couldn't wait to get back home and change back into my sweats and drink hot chocolate.

I arrived at Chateau Marmont and a beautiful twenty-year-old hostess with pouty lips and black hair looked me up and down. She didn't say anything.

"I'm meeting someone here," I said.

She turned toward the bar where a man was sitting. He nodded at her. This man, he did resemble Richard Gere. Squinty, crystal-blue eyes, gray hair, handsome. I thought maybe I'd move in with him and I wouldn't have to work. At least I wouldn't mind kissing him. I walked over. He didn't get up, just motioned for me to sit down.

"You are beautiful," he said, pouring me a glass from the half-empty bottle of wine in front of him.

We talked for a short time before he said, "Do you like anal?"

I felt my neck go stiff and lips tighten.

"Let's start over," he said. "There are things I like, and it does not mean I am gay."

"I like the Chateau Marmont," I said.

"My house is up the hill."

I knew I wouldn't be going there. Vea had said it would take a lot of interviews before I met the right match. I wasn't so sure I could keep doing this. I'd give it another week. When I got home, Chateau Marmont man texted me about the anal, and how many roses (aka money) he'd give me if I just let him. I didn't respond.

He texted again. "Just a little. Let me put a little bit in."

I deleted him.

Then I got a message from Harry, an Orthodox Jew. His email was polite and articulate. I suggested we meet at Starbucks. It was near Rilke's apartment, and knowing she was close made me feel safer.

"Too close to the Synagogue I go to," he wrote. "Let's meet at The Coffee Bean on Sunset."

The next morning Harry wrote, "I want to confirm we are to meet at 2 p.m."

I boiled two eggs, rode my bike to the gym and home, showered, dressed in a white button-up shirt and black pencil skirt.

I drove down Crescent Heights, turned left on Sunset, and pulled into the Coffee Bean lot. Across the street was The Griddle Cake, a line to get in half a block long. I thought of the times Ricardo and I had gone there for tomato-and-basil omelets, and buckwheat pancakes as big as the plate.

A man in a shiny, black Mercedes got out of his car. He was overweight, had a yarmulke on. I knew it was Harry. I imagined what he looked like naked and what it would be like to have sex with him as I checked my makeup in the rearview mirror. When I walked in, he was standing in line, and he looked right over, knowing it was me even though my face was cut off in the picture. I was the only one in black heels on a Sunday afternoon. Real couples sat at circular tables sipping coffee, eating bagels and scones, wearing flip flops and baseball caps. I wasn't hungry.

I didn't know whether to wait in line, sit at a table, go right up to Harry. I got in line, behind a blonde curly-headed woman in red shorts. He was in front of her and turned around. I hoped maybe I was mistaken, that it wasn't him.

"Alexis?" he asked.

That was the new name I'd decided on. I didn't want to go back to being Lana or Claudia.

I nodded, and he motioned for the curly girl to go ahead.

"Hi." I extended my hand.

His hand was clammy.

"What can I get you?" he asked.

"Coffee, black. Thank you."

"Why don't you find us a table?"

I chose one in the corner with a window and watched the people in line at The Griddle until Harry sat down. He got right down to business, telling me he'd had arrangements before and so had his friends at the Temple. I didn't know why he told me about his friends, I guessed maybe to reassure himself that he wasn't a bad man and that many men do it.

"I'm married and I have a daughter in Israel," he said. "I travel out of country, need woman two, three times a month. I treat you well."

The next time I met with Harry was on a Tuesday at 11:45 a.m., downtown at The Georgian. I felt embarrassed to tell him to bring champagne, but I knew I would need it even though I had never been much of a drinker. Rilke dropped me off, with Somerset sleeping in his baby seat.

"Text me when you're done," she said.

I took the elevator to the seventh floor. I hoped he was quick, and that Rilke wouldn't get bored waiting.

Harry had on a crisp white shirt, black pleated pants. He handed me an envelope, sat on the bed, and untied his polished black shoes.

"You're all I've been thinking about." He opened the champagne.

I wanted to drink the whole bottle, but I just sipped.

"So put together, you are. Everything perfect but at coffee," he frowned, "I look at your nails." He shook his head and took his yarmulke off. "What's the matter with the nails. Don't you have the money?"

I looked down at the clear polish I had put on that morning hoping it would look professional. I had never been a manicure kind of girl. I turned my back, unzipped my skirt. He undressed. His stomach hung out and there were patches of gray and black hair on it and I couldn't see his dick or balls. His white thighs had red and blue veins. Breathing heavily he walked towards me, I smelled a strange mixture of spearmint and garlic.

We were on the bed and he was kissing me with his big, too-warm lips, the coarseness of his beard against my skin. Rolling on top of me I felt crushed and that I could hardly breathe with his full weight and large belly smashed against me. His dick was so small and he never went in, just rubbed and rubbed up against me until he groaned and it was over. I was relieved it was so fast but I wasn't sure if he was really done, it seemed too easy for it to be over. But all he did was ask me, "Do you like small or big purses? I travel to Vietnam, I bring you back one."

I hoped it would be like this with him every time even if I did feel crushed by his weight. Five, six rubs and job done.

He showered, bringing his clothes into the bathroom and closing the door. I sat on the edge of the bed and waited until he came out.

"Next Wednesday," he said. "Different hotel."

He left. It was 12:43 p.m. I had made a thousand dollars. That would include the next couple of times I saw him that month. I looked at my nails and decided next time I'd get them done. I showered, dressed, and texted Rilke. "Done."

Rilke was out front in her car with Somerset awake, smiling at me from the back seat. Twenty minutes later we were at Rilke's place and I was reading *Baby Cloud* to Somerset. And then after, when he didn't want me to leave, I read him *This Train Goes Clickety Clack*.

The Iranian Sugar Daddy

I was about to give up getting a second sugar daddy when I met Omar, the short, handsome Iranian with musician's hands. We arranged to meet at The Grove.

"I'll be standing in front of the fountain in a paisley muffler," he said.

Walking towards the fountain wearing a black dress cut above the knee, I passed families sitting in a red trolley car waiting to ride to Nordstrom. Other kids stood in line to sit on Santa's knee, volunteers jingled bells for money.

Omar was standing in front of the fountain, a paisley muffler swung around his neck, hands in pockets. He was looking at me in a gentle way.

"When I saw you walking," he said as we sat at The Whisper Lounge, "I hoped it was you. Your ad impressed me. It was not like others I had read."

Omar didn't have kids and was never married. He was a financial advisor who played tennis on Saturdays and liked French films and books. And he was very formal. I liked talking to him. After drinks that night, he touched my arm, "You're cold, do you have a coat with you?"

I hadn't brought one.

"Wear mine. I'd like to buy you a little something before you go."

He helped me into his coat as we walked out of the lounge and joined the crowd of Christmas shoppers walking to Nordstrom's. He bought me a cashmere Pashmina and didn't try to kiss me when we said goodbye.

"When can I see you again?" he asked.

We arranged to meet the following week at a sushi bar on Sunset.

Speed in the Bushes

It was a few weeks after I met Omar, on a windy, Saturday morning, that something changed.

I was standing in my nightgown in the backyard. Grapefruit gouged by squirrels slumped on the overgrown ground. Bougainvillea thorns clawed at the wood fence and the vines tangled into the bushes and trees on their way up to the telephone line. My bicycle leaned against a fig tree and ferns twisted through the cobwebbed spokes.

I had been trying to quit crystal again, and it had been two weeks when I'd gotten a call from Lisa. She had called before but I hadn't picked up. This time I didn't even think about it. I was on the 10 freeway in five minutes.

Forty minutes later I was in the lingerie aisle at Ross looking for Lisa. She saw me and gave me a hug as I slipped the money into her back pocket and she handed me the baggie of crystal that was wrapped in blue tissue with a red Christmas bow. I sensed we were being watched and grabbed a pale blue robe from one of the racks and held it up in front of myself. "Perfect," I said.

I tried it on. It felt like being wrapped in rabbit. I walked to the dressing room with it and took a bra off a rack and slipped into the change room, making sure I chose one with a door that latched. I tore into the tissue. The crystals looked like organic Mediterranean salt. I prepared a line, snorted, and put the baggie in my pocket, leaving the bra and rabbit robe behind.

Now here I was, two days later with no sleep, in my backyard shaking with the wind. Barefooted and barehanded I reached towards a branch. Pink flowers fell to the ground from the trees. Purple morning glories peeked out from the bushes. A thorn pricked my finger. Prick, pick. Prick, pick. Each time a thorn pierced me I told myself to put on gloves before breaking another branch, following the bougainvillea into the bush. I was caught in the vines, tearing them apart, tearing me apart. My arms were scratched, my mouth dry. An hour passed, then two. I was on my hands and knees, then back on my feet. My shins were scratched, knees dirty, and my jaw, it was very tight.

"You go inside," I told myself. "Get water. You have to pee."

I never liked to garden before speed. Alina used to cut the grass in our front yard between the pebbled path with a pair of nail scissors. I would have to help her. The only thing I liked about that garden was when the rhubarb grew and Alina made pies out of it.

I still don't know why this day became so different than any other. At 8 p.m. I was laying on the cool black-and-pink tiles of the bathroom floor. My arms and legs stretched out wide. I was pale, nauseated, my forehead damp with cold sweat. My heart beat too fast and I couldn't get up. The scratches all up and down my arms were streaked red, like I had been attacked in the jungle. How many years had I spent in the bushes with my head down, tangled in the weeds?

My heart and head raced in rhythm to the images of my life. My mom leaving, my sister crying and clinging to my leg when I flew home every summer, brown car man, the babysitter, the nightmares. I thought about my dad and his women and his poetry, my step-mom's borscht, my little brother's dead cat. I remembered me bending over and swinging on poles for money, the drugs and the men in hotels, the decent job at the law school that I had quit and now, even though I called it sugar daddy work, being into prostitution for the third time. More images came, leading me to where I was, thirty-six, lying on the floor of my pink bathroom on a Saturday night in Los Angeles, torn red from fighting with the vines in the garden. I saw no escape.

Drinking in Therapy

I knew the escape would only begin when I stopped. And that day, I did stop the speed, and I continued to stay stopped. I think about it a lot. Why that day? Why not any other? There were so many days gardening maniacally, picking at my face for hours in the mirror, glued to the aisles at Home Depot examining screws and cabinet knobs, the hours spent at Ross looking at curtains and bras, staying up for nights, crushing lines on top of the toilet paper holder in public restrooms, typing out statistics equations in college and researching and writing papers for hours that turned into days until I was late handing them in, hiding the drugs from Ricardo and my family, the lies and stealing, the cravings while I was babysitting Somerset. Why didn't any of these days bring me to a stop?

I had never been a drinker. Had no taste for it. If there was wine at a dinner party, I took a glass just to be polite and took a sip. I thought that had something to do with being Jewish, that Jewish people didn't have drinking problems. When the speed stopped, wine is what I turned to, just one glass at dinner. Then it became two, three, and then a bottle. I would tell myself, just wait until six before drinking. Then I changed it to three, then noon, until it was all I started thinking about. I'd go to Trader Joe's and stock up on Two-Buck Chuck.

"Having a party this weekend?" the cashier would ask.

I'd go to another Trader Joe's, feeling embarrassed that I'd be recognized for buying too much wine. I knew the wine had replaced the meth. I'd try and not drink for a day, and I would get so depressed and panicked sitting there with myself that I'd end up in the Ralphs bathroom with a champagne bottle of André because I couldn't wait until I got home to drink it and take whatever I was feeling away.

Babysitting Somerset, I had managed to never do meth while I was with him, and I promised myself it would be the same with the drinking. There was no question. I'd make it until I got home and then drink. One day, I was in the fruit section at Whole Foods and Somerset was asleep in his carriage holding his basketball. He always liked to hold that thing when he slept. I picked out a few nectarines, decided to wash one in case Somerset woke up on the way home and was hungry. I went to the water fountain, next to the bathroom. As I walked towards the fountain, I passed the wine section. It wasn't even a thought. I had been craving it all day but I knew I couldn't, not with Somerset there. I grabbed the first bottle of wine I saw, a forty-five-dollar one. I walked past the fountain with that bottle and the stroller, straight into the ladies' room. I locked the door behind us. Somerset was still sleeping and I faced the stroller away from where I sat on the toilet and opened that bottle and drank. The basketball in Somerset's arms fell to the floor and he started to cry. I got his ball and put it back into his arms. He didn't stop crying.

I knew I needed help. I wanted to talk to Rilke but I was scared, she had never known about me going back on meth.

And the drinking, she thought it was just a phase. But I knew that it wasn't, it was just a replacement for the drugs.

I started seeing a therapist at The Maple Counseling Center on Wilshire Boulevard in Beverly Hills. The center worked on a sliding scale basis. My appointment was Tuesdays at 12 p.m. The therapist was warm and older and I wanted to hide under her armpit. For the first couple of months I was able to not drink before my appointment but as soon as therapy was over, at 12:55 I'd walk across the street to CVS, get a bottle of red wine, and go into the bathroom. I kept a wine opener in my purse.

Then I started not being able to wait until after. I'd go to CVS, get a bottle of wine, go into the bathroom, sit on the toilet and drink from the bottle. I hid what was left in the trash under dirty tissue telling myself I would not come back after therapy to finish it. But an hour later I was back in the bathroom looking for the bottle in the trash. Sometimes, when I couldn't use the CVS bathroom because an employee was hovering around the entrance, I'd use the center's bathroom. I'd sit on the toilet, take out my wine opener, hold the bottle between my legs, and pull. If another woman was in the stall next to me or washing her hands, I'd wait to uncork it until they left. When they took too long washing their hands and checking their makeup in the mirror, I'd flush the toilet and pull the cork out as fast as I could.

One day my therapist said something to me. I'll never forget that day. I parked in the underground lot of CVS. Took the back stairway that smelled of urine and chlorine up into the drugstore that I had been to every Tuesday for the last three months, never to buy lip gloss or a musical greeting card but always cheap red wine. That day, there was a long line and I stood there at 11:45 a.m. with my bottle behind a woman who had a cart full of diapers and mountain spring water and a baby on her hip. The baby turned to look at me, didn't blink or move, just stared like a doll. I tried to smile at the baby as I put the bottle I had in my hand behind my back, holding it by the neck. My thoughts went to that doll my childhood friend Emily got for her sixth birthday and how I had turned off the lights and thrown the doll out the second story window. All the little girls running to the window, looking out at the porcelain legs that were shattered on the pavement.

I thought about how in fifteen minutes I'd cross the street to Maple Counseling, walk into my therapist's windowless office and sit on her floral couch. I didn't like floral prints and I didn't like it when my therapist said, "I want you to imagine yourself at six, you are in your pink- and white-checkered shorts swinging on the swing in the park and the man in the car called out to you."

I didn't know what to say to her. I just looked at her and my breath became shallow, always the breath, I couldn't get it in, not a whole, deep breath.

"Where do you feel it in your body?" she'd ask.

"I feel it everywhere. My body freezes and I can't get air in."

"I want you to sit with that feeling, try not to shut it out."

But I wanted to shut it out. I wanted to not think about that day and for her to stop asking me how I felt. I wanted to talk about something else, but another part of me wanted to stay and talk and feel things that were swallowed deep for too long.

I was still in line at the CVS with that baby looking at me. I left the line and walked to the back of the store and pretended to look at the selection of earth-friendly garbage bags. I made sure no one was looking and entered into the employees-only black double doors and went into the bathroom. I knew the store had cameras and my heart was beating fast. I locked the door and sat on the toilet. I told myself, just a little before therapy, she'll never know. I drank half the bottle and someone tried to open the door. I flushed the toilet and reached into the big black bin of garbage and hid the bottle under the dirty paper towels. Then I ran the water, washed my hands and opened the door to a young girl in a blue uniform with a nametag on her chest, Candy.

"This is an employee-only bathroom," she said.

"I'm sorry," I said. "I had to pee badly."

No one had ever said anything to me before about using the bathroom, but I was always scared they would and that someone would see me on camera, but it didn't stop me. Even when I was nine and the cops brought me home after I had been caught stealing ballet tights and a Butterfinger, I went right on stealing. Mostly Bonnie Bell grape and strawberry lip-smackers, the fat kind, for the girls at school. I had hoped I'd get a friend that way. I'd see their eyes light up whenever I gave them one and watch as they rubbed that grape on their lips while the teacher covered the chalkboard with plus and minus signs that I didn't understand. The Bonnie Bell's didn't make me their friends. At lunch I'd hide under the bleachers, and I continued to hide there until I graduated high school.

Now, almost thirty years later, I was still stealing and still hiding. The grape-flavored gloss had become wine and the bleachers had become restrooms all over Los Angeles; Ralphs, Goodwill, the law school, and then the drug store in Beverly Hills before therapy.

I left CVS that day, walked across the street to Maple Counseling, took the elevator one floor below the lobby where the center was underground without windows and into the waiting room where a few children sat at a circular table coloring, their parents sitting in steel folding chairs along the wall, waiting to be called into their fifty-minute therapy sessions. I looked at a girl of about six with yellow ribbons tied on the ends of two braids and I wondered why she was brought for therapy and why my dad and Alina didn't take me when I was six and started having baby nightmares. Maybe it wasn't so common for kids to be in therapy back then, maybe it was too expensive, or maybe they thought having my head wired up and tested for sleep patterns was good enough, especially since the nightmares went away after that. Sitting there waiting for my own therapist, I thought that maybe one day I should ask my dad about the day in the park and what he was told when he came back from India. Did he call and tell my real mom, or did Alina? I decided I should first talk about it in therapy.

My therapist called me in. I followed her down a narrow hallway of closed doors, watched her long skirt float around her legs and into the room. I sat on that floral couch opposite her. She crossed her legs.

"How are you today?" she asked.

I tried to look her in the eye and say something but I found myself staring at the tassels of her red scarf while my eyes filled with tears and the tassels blurred into a red cloud.

The wine made me cry easily. I needed more. I wanted therapy to be over even though I had just sat down. At the same time I wanted to stay. I knew I needed help, not just with the drugs and alcohol but with everything. I'd never felt I knew how to live like other people were living. Watching them they seemed to know how to go about things, to get through the day and do things like get their oil checked, go to work, and do the dishes after dinner, all the things that make up a life. I knew that this couldn't be the case for everyone. That some people who I imagined had it together really didn't. But I wanted to be someone who did know how to cope and I knew that's why I had chosen therapy and was sitting in that small room across from a fifty-something-year-old woman in a flowing skirt with brown shiny eyes. I wanted her to help me to feel like I could function, that I mattered and had a purpose.

Right then I felt her eyes strong on me and heard her voice, words that seemed to come out slow, almost a whisper, but she wasn't whispering or talking extra slow.

"I understand you want to be here, but we can't continue to do the work if you come in here like this."

My cheeks turned hot red and my heart started beating so fast. I wondered how my therapist knew. I thought I was acting normal and that nobody could tell and that the breath mints I always ate hid the smell. Even though I hadn't been seeing her long, I didn't want to lose her. And drinking while I was with Somerset in the stroller at Whole Foods, I had crossed what I felt was the ultimate line. It was one of the hardest things I ever had to do. But something changed in me. It was like the day with speed only this time it was the wine and I knew that I would need to stop everything.

The tears came down my cheeks and I was shaking, trembling, I couldn't get any breath in. The more I tried to breathe the harder it was to get any air. I couldn't control how my body was reacting. A damp chill dropped through, my hot cheeks turned pale, and sweat formed on my forehead. I kept gasping for air. I had never felt so scared, so much like I was going crazy and dying at the same time. I felt like I did that day in the movie theater years earlier when I watched the scene with the two-year-old boy pressing his face against the window crying out "Mom, Mom," as she walked down the pathway without turning back.

I wasn't able to drive home that day from therapy. I don't remember what my therapist said or how I got up and walked out of her office but the image that remains is me sitting in my car in the underground lot of CVS pressing numbers on my phone, and the sound of Rilke's voice on the other end. I didn't have to say one word. She knew something was wrong and she was there. I left my car in the lot and Rilke picked me up. She put her arms around me, Somerset was in the backseat, his bright two-year-old face, hair curly in all directions. "Auntie," he said, holding out his fat little arms.

Friendly House

Those early days of trying to get sober, I didn't think I could do it. Every morning I'd get out of bed and press the red button on my two-cup Mr. Coffee maker and wait, staring out the window at the fig tree. Drip, drip, drip. I loved that fig tree. Just wanted to lay there and stare at it all day and wait until night when I could get my head to the pillow sober. Head to pillow. That's all I had to do. Nothing else mattered except not using or drinking that day. Sometimes I'd get under the covers in the middle of the day and try and sleep the hours away but the hours were always there. It had been years since I had lived sober. It was all new, learning how to be in the world without turning to speed or alcohol. The cravings were bad.

My therapist told me about a place in Koreatown where women who have drug and alcohol problems have meetings and they share their stories and try and help each other get better.

Friendly House. The first all-girls residential rehab, since 1951. A big, fat house next to a Korean church on Normandie. It was the only house on a narrow street surrounded by apartment buildings with gated doors that needed painting. Cracked windows and unwanted stained mattresses set out front on the sidewalk waiting to be taken away. People sat on the steps outside in baggy shorts and white tube socks pulled high. It was always hard to park, and the signs said no parking until seven, so at around six thirty people would sit in their faded 1988 Hondas with their windows rolled down watching for parking enforcement until seven so they could get a spot for the night.

I'd circle around and it seemed like I always ended up getting the same spot on Oxford, a couple streets over, in front of the sacred shrine of Mary or somebody. I don't know who. It was a structure made out of wood set in between those ugly apartments, and it had a pointed roof and three wooden walls. No front wall. You could just walk right in and kneel in front of Mary and maybe light a candle because there were lots of candles with Jesus Christ on them, the tall skinny kinds like you see at the Dollar Store. Dried orange gerberas and yellow roses and sometimes a few brown bananas beneath her. I never saw bananas at church before but I remember seeing them at the feet of Krishna at an Indian Temple, but Krishna's bananas were yellow: ripe, no bruises. Sometimes I thought maybe I should pick a flower and place it there and make a wish or something but I never did.

I'd walk over to Friendly House and up the big front yard that had patches of grass missing, and the house cat, skinny and gray with white feet, he would always be sitting there on the first step looking at me before running away under a car. I don't think that cat liked all us girls coming around, or even the girls that lived there. It was a lot of us coming in and out. Getting thirty days clean and starting to look maybe a little better and then they'd leave and sometimes they'd come back and try again but more often they didn't come back.

That first time I went I sat in the back and cried. Right away

I felt like it was a place where it was okay not to be okay. I don't remember what one person said the first night except for this woman. She came right up to me with her burgundy wig and deep, scratchy voice and shook her finger at me, a long purple nail kind of curved it was so long with sparkles on it.

She looked me straight in the eye, "Honey, you don't ever have to use or drink again no matter what."

No one ever said something like that to me before and it just seemed like, I don't know, but there was something about that purple nail and what she said that had me come back.

The End of Harry

The day after that first meeting at Friendly House, I had already arranged to meet the Orthodox Jew at The Saint George Hotel downtown on Figueroa at 11 a.m. That was our day, the third Tuesday of every month. There was something about that day, putting my black little suit and heels on, painting my nails red, waiting for them to dry, staring out my window, a real pretty window, the old kind that opens wide into the room with the wood crossing in the middle, I was looking out it at the fig tree and this squirrel was trying to eat one of the figs or take it away with him to his family. I don't know, but he looked like a frustrated squirrel and he was going for the biggest fig. I just wanted to pick it and put it on a plate for him or walk it on over to where that squirrel's family was. I was watching him and I just didn't know how I was not going to drink with that man and his big belly with all those blue and red veins crisscrossing on it and I just knew that if I kept sleeping with him, I would drink.

That day at The Saint George, I knew it would be the last time. He took his yarmulke off, didn't say a thing, most the time that's the way he was, quiet like that, and then he just kind of put himself on top of me and it was all over fast just like the first time I was with him, and I was relieved. He put that yarmulke back on his head then his black socks and walked across the room with his loose belly all out there, exposed. I just lay under the sheet naked watching him as he put the rest of his clothes back on, set a white envelope next to the TV, and walked out.

Inside the envelope was a check. Normally he gave me cash, and I wondered why he would do that, give me a check with his real name on it. On the top corner was his address, 616 N. McCadden Ave. One block from where I lived. After that, whenever I rode my turquoise bicycle with the stenciled white flowers by the synagogue a few blocks away, I wondered if Harry was under one of those black robes and fur hats. And what about the other men in their fur hats and the girls they met in hotels before matzo ball soup or after Shabbat dinner?

Harry texted me the following month.

I didn't answer.

Omar was different. He never pushed for sex, and the only time we were ever together was the third time I saw him. He put on Sade and made me an Iranian dinner. There was no wine and as I tried to eat the lamb stew and chickpeas I couldn't imagine sleeping with Omar sober. Drinking with Harry made it bearable.

Taking my hand and leading me to his stark bedroom we undressed and got under the thin gray covers. Omar seemed less interested in the sex than just wanting to hold me and lay still, and all I could think about was when would the cuddling be over. In a way having sex was easier. There was an end point. With cuddling, his body curled into mine, time felt even longer, and without anything to drink I felt anxious. I kept thinking about the red wine going down my throat, the warm sensation that came over me, and a kind of foggy slumber that helped me drift somewhere else. Anywhere else but here with Omar breathing in my ear, the scent of saffron and lamb.

It was like talking to the men at the strip club. It was easier to get right to it, give the three-minute private dance and be done, the man would be gone. But Omar didn't seem made for sex. Maybe that's why he didn't push for it.

I didn't understand him. Why he was patient and wanted to do things for me like taking me grocery shopping. He'd drive all the way from Sherman Oaks in his black waxed Audi to take me shopping on Sundays at Trader Joe's, filling the cart with coffee, dish soap, and vine tomatoes, not the cheap Roma ones that I usually got. He'd help me inside with groceries, leaving half the month's rent on the table and kissing me goodbye on the cheek.

He also took me shopping for clothes. I never cared much about fashion or buying new clothes. Just being in a department store felt like work to me and gave me a backache. But Omar liked buying clothes for me.

"I'm taking you to a new boutique for a dress," he'd say, opening the car door for me.

He'd buy me things that I never wore except when I saw him. I wanted to tell him what I really needed was money to pay the phone bill or something practical, like a new hot plate for my makeshift kitchen, or running shoes, but I didn't feel right saying that to him.

Once a week we went for sushi on Larchmont. One time the hostess took our picture. The next time we came the picture was on the wall, the two of us smiling, Omar's arm around me, sushi chef's hat in the background and under the picture in black ink 'Happy couple share fresh squid'.

As time went on I knew he really did care for me. And I liked him, the way he smelled, talking to him, going out to dinner once a week with him. But I didn't feel anything for him romantically. The thing of it was, being with him felt like more than placing an ad on Craigslist and having an arrangement with a sugar daddy. I felt like I was deceiving him, that it wasn't right to continue seeing him since I didn't feel the same way as he did, that I was using him. And I was, but I was too scared to not have his help.

Tailwaggers

2008

I went to Friendly House every Thursday night and sat with other girls in rows of chairs in front of a fireplace. A picture-book kind of fireplace where Santa could come down the chimney. A fairytale fireplace, only this one was real, and in December it would be all set up with tinsel and stockings hung with the names of the girls living in the house. Some of those girls with their names on the red stockings, they'd stay, and others would go. Some back to Skid Row, others to gated homes in Bel Air, but most of the time, no matter where they went, if they left it never went well, and some even ended up dead. I didn't want to be one of those girls.

The thing is, you never knew who was going to make it or go back out there and drink and get high. Like this one girl, looking at her all hollowed out and scared it was hard to imagine she'd put a day sober together. But she did, and eventually she even starting working at Friendly House. She was maybe nineteen, twenty. She was extra pretty, with dark hair and brown eyes that slanted up and a real cute little figure. I didn't know there was anything pretty about her at first. She had been living in a box or a tent on Skid Row and shooting heroin. She arrived with no shoes on, and her feet were torn-up-looking with scabs, and her toenails didn't look right. Kind of twisted-looking and brown, and her hair was all matted down to her head. She had circles under her eyes that looked extra dark against her pale skin and she was wearing a torn up tee shirt that said, Scooby Doo: I Love You.

That girl was bathed and put to bed and slept for three days straight, but after that she had to get up like all the other girls in the house and follow the routine. Like going to group where the girls talked about their feelings and then did double scrub and baked. There was always a cake being made.

Every week when I came back for the meeting she was there, and after a while we started making the coffee and setting up the chairs together because everyone had a commitment. There was the Countess of Lighting, the Friendly Phone-List Princess, and the Duchess of Court Cards (for the girls who were court-ordered to be there and had to have their yellow slip signed for the judge).

As the Scooby Doo girl and I set up chairs we started to talk. Turned out when she was little her mom also left. After that we started sitting next to each other all the time. I saw a younger version of myself in her, and I thought about all the years I had been tangled in the weeds of my life and I hoped she would get out earlier than I did. I felt motherly towards her, maybe how Bunni and Anna felt towards Rilke and me when we were kids. Since I knew at a young age I never wanted children, I always thought about how one day maybe I could be an Anna or a Bunni in a girl's life.

At seven o'clock, after the meeting was set up, everyone would be seated on the floral couches and wood chairs with high backs and cushions with different designs, paisleys and kittens and Santa Claus. Those cushions, they kind of depressed me. So did the floral couches. But then the meeting would start and the speaker, who was always a different lady with a bunch of years sober, she'd talk about her life drinking and getting high and how she'd managed to stay clean, and most the time, by the end I forgot all about the cushions.

Going there, hearing all those stories and talking with the girls, somehow it helped me to not drink or use, and I started to put some sober days together, and those days turned into months. They were the hardest months I can remember. I'd wake up with this gripping dread and anxiety of the hours before me. How was I going to get through the day? I couldn't tolerate being alone with myself, and at the same time I felt paralyzed to get up and do anything. I'd sit on the couch, stare at the wood floor that needed sweeping, then at the blank page of my journal. I'd think of the lady with the purple fingernail and hear her scratchy voice, "Honey, you don't need to drink or use no matter what."

Then I'd write a few words down and how many days sober I had, and the next day when I didn't know how I was going to get my head to the pillow sober, I'd stare at the entry from the previous day. 'Day 22 – 1 p.m. Nine-hours until bedtime.' I'd hold onto the fact I made it through that day and maybe I could for another day again.

As the days passed, I started to feel better, just a little bit. I started to not hate myself as much for the choices I had made and everything I felt dirty about. I felt less alone, and the more stories I heard at Friendly House, the more connected and less alone I felt. I realized everyone had a story like this one woman, Honey, a Hawaiian lesbian.

"A model," she said. "I was on the cover of three magazines

at the same time and I was drinking every day, I was at my bottom."

I remembered her from the cover of *Vogue* and how I'd looked at the glossy page with her smiling back at me. I couldn't believe it. This woman who at the time I thought had it all and couldn't at all be unhappy, let alone in despair like I was, here she was sharing that during that time she had been at her bottom.

I knew one could never tell what was really going on with a person from the outside. That being on the cover of a magazine or having a bestseller didn't equal happiness. But to actually hear it in person made it real and confirmed that ultimately, peace of mind was an internal job. And that's all I ever wanted, to be able to sit with myself and be OK, but it was something I'd never thought possible. And now for the first time, there was a small part of me that thought maybe I'd been wrong.

"I was sixteen when I ran away from home," she shared. "A one-way ticket to California. I got myself a job at Disneyland as Snow White. Every morning I'd powder my face and arms all white and pale and color my lips ruby red. I wore a pale blue satin dress that puffed out in all directions with a skinny white patent-leather belt and patent-leather white heels, and me and my seven dwarfs would go off to our seven-hour shift at the dwarf's cottage. Sleepy, Grumpy, Dopey, all of them with their tin lunch cases and me with a satin pink purse. In that purse I always had a flask of whiskey."

"One day, some of the dwarfs got drunk with me and I drank even more than usual and did one too many twirls and got fired on the basis of being a sloppy Snow White."

Turned out, that lady with the purple fingernail who I met that first night, she'd worked at Disneyland too. She was Goofy. A six-foot-two Goofy. She had all this room under her costume.

"Like a tent," she said. "It was perfect. I had my arms free because the costume arms were fake so I could crack open a beer under there and put on my headset and dance and get real loose. I had to go to the bathroom all the time for another beer since I could only hold two at a time under the costume. I had my replenishing system down. The janitor of that bathroom for the Mickey Mouse crew, he drank, too. I'd bring in a six-pack and so would he and we'd hide it in the garbage can. Since it was an employee bathroom it had a lock on it. We had it down perfect. Then they went and promoted me to Tarzan, which made no sense since I was a terrible Goofy, and it messed up my whole system and I got fired."

I heard other stories too. Like this one politician lady, she shared about going into Pavilions and drinking in the bathroom and putting steaks and Advil in her purse.

"I just thought they were overpriced," she said.

I don't know why, but that politician lady took a liking to me, and she wasn't warm to too many people. Maybe it was on account of her not having a good relationship with her own daughter. One night, when I was sharing about how hard it was to get through the day clean, she put her arm around me and said,

"Honey, we've all been there."

And then she took me for lasagna. She became the new Bunni and Anna in my life. She took me to see her horses, and that was something special because she didn't take anyone to see her horses. Cleopatra and Omaha. She loved those horses even though they threw her off, at least Cleopatra did. And that lady, she was like seventy, and sometimes came to the meeting pretty beat-up looking with a broken arm and neck brace. But she kept riding those horses. She took a picture that I saved of me standing with Omaha feeding him a really big carrot, the biggest I ever saw. That picture, looking at it, made me feel special. I looked at that picture a lot.

Most of the time, I didn't feel anything like special. But as time went on, little by little, I started to feel a little OK. Like when I went to the grocery store I could look the checker or the bag boy in the eye because I didn't have something I didn't pay for in my purse and I hadn't been locked up in the store bathroom drinking wine or doing lines on the toilet paper dispenser. I even remember the very last thing I stole. Piña colada gum. Not the whole pack. A couple pieces. I opened it while I was walking around, I just wanted to see what it tasted like, so that's what I did and I chewed at it, decided it was no good and then pretended to look at the ground beef and put the rest of that piña colada under it.

The next night I shared about what I had done at that meeting.

The lady with the horses came up to me after and said, "Honey, the last steak I ever stole was twenty years ago when I first got sober and I'll tell you what I did, I went back into that store and paid for it."

And the next day, that's what I did. I bought that piña colada gum and then I put that same pack back and left, and that was the very last time I ever stole even one thing.

I also shared at that meeting about being a call girl, a stripper, and all the dirty things about my using and drinking that I felt bad about. I never felt judged and nobody ever told me what to do, people just shared their own experiences and what helped them.

When I had about three months sober I told the politician lady about Omar, and how I didn't feel good about it.

"I can't keep taking money from him. I've got to get a job, but I don't know what, and I can't, I just can't be shut in an office for eight hours, and I'm a terrible waitress."

"Honey," she said, "What you need is a simple sober job. A job where you don't have to think, you just show up and learn to be on time, honest, and accountable."

"And make ten dollars an hour?" I asked.

"I asked the same thing when I was new but I promise, as long as you stay sober, it will all work out."

It didn't feel like it would, but I knew I couldn't keep doing what I was doing, so that's what I did. I started working at a friend's pet food and supply store, Tailwaggers. It was five minutes from my place, on Fairfax in between Shorty's and Genghis Cohen, an old Chinese restaurant with red leather booths, dim lighting, and bluesy singers.

Five times a week I stocked Merrick Working Dog Stew and Grammy's Pot Pie, mopped the floors, and arranged the Swarovski studded dog collars. The guy who I worked with, it turned out he had eight months sober off of meth, and we shared stories about going to Rite Aid and looking at thumbtacks for hours at 4 a.m., hanging out with our dealers like Kasper and Turtle and taking apart doorknobs. While we talked, the whole time we kept stocking those dog cans, trying to stay clean another day.

Happy Couple

I had been working at Tailwaggers for a few months when Omar took me to a one-woman show about Janis Joplin that I wanted to see. On the way he said, "You are not like other girls I have met who want Porsches and designer purses. You, you are different. Special you are."

Hand-in-hand we entered the theater on Santa Monica Boulevard across from Dragonfly and 7-Eleven. Streetwalkers were walking back and forth in front of Donut Stop in high heels and backpacks. I felt my shoulders tighten up.

We sat in faded velvet theater seats. Omar put his small arm around me. It felt heavy on my shoulder. I crossed my legs. The chair creaked. I wanted to scratch my nose but my arms, hands felt frozen with Omar next to me. This man knew I lived in a kitchen-less room with a hot plate, that I sold Working Dog Stew and Grammy's Pot Pie for work, and that I placed an ad on Craigslist for a sugar daddy and that I probably had other men.

But I didn't, and Omar, he was still there. The dog food, the no sex, the hot plate. We went to the sushi restaurant on Larchmont after the play. We ordered octopus and rainbow rolls.

At the table across from us sat a couple. The woman was smiling at her man. He had a black mustache and there was something pinkish on it, salmon or strawberry. She leaned in with her napkin and wiped at it.

Omar put his warm hand on top of mine.

"You like where I live?" he asked.

I imagined myself lying next to Omar on a treeless street in Sherman Oaks: a two bedroom apartment, white carpets, white leather couch, too many white cabinets, steel gray blinds, low ceiling.

I looked at the couple across from us. Who loved who more? Did she always love him, or did she grow into it?

Why didn't Omar own a house in Hancock Park on a fat street with shade, wood floors, and bougainvillea?

"You could go back to school," he said. "I could get you a new car."

I was driving a 1987 Ford Taurus wagon and the back end was smashed in. It looked like half a car. My neighbor had left a note on the windshield.

"Don't park your jalopy in front of my house."

I had gotten into an accident months ago but it still ran pretty good and it was too much money to fix and I couldn't bring myself to ask Omar to help pay for it. Whenever I went to the gym I parked a block away so no one would see. Nobody in LA drives half a car.

I thought about what kind I would get. A white Mini Cooper with a stripe, a black truck. And school, I could get an MFA, quit the dog store, get my nails done every week and my hair straightened, and new running shoes, and lots of white socks.

"We have grown close," he said, taking my hand in his. "I am in love with you."

I looked up at the picture of us that was still tacked on the wall with other couples. "Happy couple." My jaw felt tight. I wasn't hungry and I didn't know what to say. That night he dropped me off at home and drove back alone to Sherman Oaks. I washed my face, took off the dress he had bought me and put on a big blue robe. Then I plugged in my hot plate and warmed almond milk with a little cinnamon.

The next day I would stock dog food and tell Omar that I cared for him but I couldn't do this anymore.

Omar and the Bulldog

Without Omar's help, I worried about how I was going to pay my rent more and more. Every couple of weeks I would get a text from him.

"I hope you are doing okay. Please let me know if you need anything, any help at all."

"Thank you so much," I'd text back. "All is well on my end and I am getting by."

All didn't feel well. Telling him I was OK for money when I wasn't sure if I could get by that month, there were so many times I thought I'd break down and see him. Or even see Harry. All it would take was an hour.

I remember one day, it had been about two months since I had stopped seeing Omar, I was working at the dog store behind the register in the uniform red tee shirt with a dog paw over my heart. A guy with brown spiky hair and a studded belt walked in. I wished I wasn't wearing the shirt. The guy had this bulldog with him on a black leather leash. The two of them circled the store. The dog lifted up his back leg and peed next to a carpeted cat tower and they left. As I took a wad of paper towels and natural disinfectant spray and cleaned up the pee I thought about the eleven dollars an hour I was making and how, by the end of my shift I would have made forty-two dollars.

I broke down in the bathroom crying. I wanted to use, to drink, to not deal with anything. I thought about Harry, how I could just go back to him and make a thousand dollars. Or Omar. I could go back to school, not worry about rent, get a new car. But I knew I couldn't live in Sherman Oaks with no trees and a low ceiling. I thought about Friendly House and all the stockings with the names of the girls that hung around the fireplace and how the ones who stayed sober, their lives got better, and the girls who didn't ended up with a needle in the arm, a bottle in their hand, or dead at a seedy motel on Sunset Boulevard. I imagined putting fresh mint in a glass bottle like the woman I admired in college, the people I watched at The Farmers Market who bought peonies for themselves not just on their birthday but on ordinary Sundays, and the ones comfortable enough within themselves to sit in solitude. I knew in my heart I needed to write. To really write. And to do so, that's what it would take. Being comfortable enough to sit long enough in front of a blank page and fill the page. If I went back to my old way of living, I knew just how easy it would be to slip away from the little bit of integrity I was beginning to form.

I went back to stocking one can of Grammy's Pot Pie at a time until the whole rack was nicely stacked. Then I went home, turned on the light at my wooden desk, and put a word down.

Writing Among the Eucalyptus Trees

I am visiting my dad. We are in his poetry studio. An octagonal room surrounded by eucalyptus trees, long windows on all sides, wood-beamed ceiling, a skylight in the middle. I sleep here on a mat in a blue-and-red sleeping bag, pretend I'm camping under the stars.

On the wall, a large black-and-white photograph of us under an arch of huge pine trees. His back to the camera. I am in a canvas carrier. You can see my head resting on his shoulder. One of my hands is on his other shoulder. His black hair full and wild. Under the photograph my dad is sitting at his desk. I sit in an old rocking chair, feet on one of the pile of books.

I am reading a chapter to him that I wrote about my mom being in my life now. How, ever since she started seeing Peter and offered to help me through college, a bond was formed that I had wanted my whole life. She visits every spring, writes me letters, and when I call her every week she asks if I need anything and asks questions about my life. I never thought this would happen. I had feared that it would end. That she would be gone again. But she's still here. She is more mom than she's ever been.

My dad listens and says not one word. I look out the window: a deer is standing there, staring at us. My dad turns his head. I stop reading from the pages and it's just the deer, my dad and me, for a moment.

Now, in the early evening we walk under the redwoods like long ago. I have my hand in his, breathing, walking, listening for forest sounds.

Acknowledgments

My father, for the gift of the written word. My mother, for your love of the written word. And both, for your belief in me as a writer. My stepfather, who knew I was writer before I did and who, when I began to write, read and edited every story I wrote. David Kline, your encouragement, and belief in my writing. Alexis, for your loving nudge to connect with John Coetzee. Nicholas, Irina, Kamala, Robin. And lastly, Danté. Who appears in just about every chapter and who has, from the beginning— I know. You know. Grateful.

Jill Schary Robinson. Who, without, I'm not sure this book would have been written. Jill saw the book I was afraid to tell. The countless Sundays editing on your couch near the 405 slicing words, piecing together fragments of a life until I could feel it breathe on my own.

Grateful to Jerry Brennan. For your belief in *Strip*, your patience, hours of editing, and for bringing this book out into the world. Immense gratitude to Tortoise Books. And, for the gift of speaking the same 'language'.

Grateful to Sheryl Johnston. My publicist. Who, from the first conversation, I knew I wanted to work with. Thank you, Sheryl. Such a gift you are.

Jamie Maclean at Coombs Moylett MacLean Literary Agency in London. For your belief in *Strip* from the very beginning. Your early readings, edits, and endless support. For the gift of finding a home for my work at *Erotic Review*. And for becoming my first agent.

Christina McDowell and Claire Titelman. Immense gratitude for our writing circle. The consistency, encouragement, feedback, accountability, and most of all, friendship.

Wimpole Street Writers. For the many nights at Jill's supporting each other's work over rye bread and salted caramel ice cream.

Christina Simos and Babette Ison. For everything. Christina, for suggesting that I 'just start by writing five minutes a day.' Babette, for showing me how to Stand Tall. For both of you who without, I would not be the woman I am today. Tinna Flores, for the honor of getting to hold your hand.

Grateful to Louie Mandrapilias for coming to the rescue. My soul brother.

Grateful to my friends, my support, my heart, my trudging, and more often than not, skipping buddies. Anna Stookey, Tanna Moontaro, Rose Black, The L 5 (Carlos Portugal, Rob Hudson, Peter Christman, Paolo Piu), John Griffiths, Bobby Burnett, Jad Nickola Najjar, Corey Powell, Michon Roth, Maxine Nunes, Antonia Blyth, Michael Wolfe, Gregory & Lawrence Zarian, Byron Potts, Sandy Hutchens, Christopher Harrity, Shawn Estebo,

John Carlos Frey, Coeleen Kiebert, and Kate Alexander (I'll never forget taking the train to NYC at the age of 19 to visit you and spending our time reading Whitman's "Song of Myself.")

Friendly House, Happy Hour Family, Los Angeles LGBT Center, WWS, Pomo Group, Sam Fleishman, Arianna Jeret at *YourTango*, David Rocklin at Roar Shack, and Paul Massignani at *Hypertext*. For the literary journals that published excerpts. *Arts & Letters*, *Other Voices*, *Rozlyn: Short Fiction by Women Writers*, *Erotic Review*, *Hypertext*, *Word Riot*, and *YourTango*.

Grateful to J.M. Coetzee, Rob Roberge, Melissa Broder, Amy Dresner, Christina McDowell, Jill Schary Robinson, Ben Stein, and Bernadette Murphy. Grateful to you all for the honor of your blurbs.

Rachael Crawford. My heart for the past thirty-three years.

Margaret Hickman, Lynne Hostein, and Eve Siegel. For helping me to learn to tolerate sitting in the hours and in turn, being able to sit with the words. It has taken years. I could ask for no greater gift.

And lastly, my HP. For the absolute abundance in my life.

About the Author

Hannah Sward's work has appeared in numerous literary journals such as *Arts & Letters*, *Yemassee*, *Halcoyne* (Black Mountain Press), *Red Wheelbarrow*, *Porter Gulch Review*, *Other Voices* (Canada), *Anthology of The Mad Ones*, *Milk*, *Alimentum*, *Anthology of Women Writers*, *Hypertext*, *Pig Iron Malt*, *Pindeldboz*, *Nerve Cowboy*, *Afternoon*, *Wimpole Street Writers*, *Lickerish Library* and *Word Riot*. She has been a regular contributor at *Erotic Review* since 2015 and was Editor and Columnist at *Third Street Villager Los Angeles* and a contributor at *The Fix* and *YourTango*. Hannah is on the board of Right To Write Press, a nonprofit that supports emerging writers who are incarcerated. She lives in Los Angeles. Find out more at hannahsward.com.

About Tortoise Books

Slow and steady wins in the end, even in publishing. Tortoise Books is dedicated to finding and promoting quality authors who haven't yet found a niche in the marketplace—writers producing memorable and engaging works that will stand the test of time. Learn more at www.tortoisebooks.com, find us on Facebook, or follow us on Twitter: @TortoiseBooks

CPSIA information can be obtained
at www.ICGtesting.com
Printed in the USA
JSHW021600290722
28712JS00003B/4

9 781948 954679